Prairie, Mountain, Desert, and Beyond

Other books by the author

Short Grass Prairie
Home
Leaving Lakehouse
Internal Landscape, External Reality,
Hunting, Fishing, Life, in Essay and Story

Prairie, Mountain, Desert, and Beyond

Richard Reitz

iUniverse, Inc.
Bloomington

Prairie, Mountain, Desert, and Beyond

iUniverse books may be ordered through booksellers or by contacting:

iUniverse
1663 Liberty Drive
Bloomington, IN 47403
www.iuniverse.com
1-800-Authors (1-800-288-4677)

ISBN: 978-1-4620-1761-4 (pbk)
ISBN: 978-1-4620-1762-1 (clth)
ISBN: 978-1-4620-1763-8 (ebk)

Printed in the United States of America

iUniverse rev. date: 05/12/2011

CONTENTS

Thanks to Marylou Barrows for careful copy reading.
Covers and photographs by author

For family and friends, who listened, read,
and offered encouragement in my
making of poems.

Prairie

Sandhills

I suppose I should tell you before you go
That people get lost out there in the hills.
We manage to find almost all of them though.
They always complain that the hills are alike,
The usual comparison is like waves of the sea,
Though I don't see the sea as a place for a hike,
Or sandhills either, if you ask what I like.

But you'll be all right if you follow advice:
Keep track of the sun, which is usually out;
Stay clear of the cactus though its blooms look nice.
Remember the fences will run north and south,
Or they run east and west; and keep track of windmills.
I can't say you'll find much if you thought this a drouth,
So don't you come back looking down at the mouth.

Topographic

Two, swift, Western rivers flowing east
Against that early human stream now kept
By granite markers in remembrance
Delineate the center of our map.
But if the past we are moves east and west
The past we knew was always north and south,
Though not beyond what some would call locale.
If you are one to need specifics here,
The rivers are the Plattes, but I have doubts
A map would be of help except for that.

Our habit was to call those on the north
Northsiders, unless—when we were playful,
Because they used the land there as it was,
Not changing it except to fence and graze,
And lived so far from town they lived on beans—
We called them "wrinkle-bellies" (to ourselves).
Those on the south were Southsiders, of course.
(When I was young we lived between the Plattes.)

Between the Plattes the land was used both ways,
Most often in simple combination
That made both hay and corn to feed the cows
But had some sandhill pasture near the place.
I guess it should be said to make it clear,
That no one ever called a ranch a ranch
Or farm a farm when he was living there:
It was "the place," as cattle were "the cows."

My saying this is just a way to show
That symbols are important on a map,
Especially when things happen later on
To change the common view of how things were.
They tell me, for example, how at first
To call a man cowboy was an insult,
Indicating a shiftless, ne'r-do-well,
Run-of-the-mill lack of character
More given to loafing than working, with
None of the usual respect for things
Plain farmers or even stock-farmers had.
This was usually said in metaphor,
Like the one about grandfather's hired man
Who cleaning out the basement of the house
Hauled out the chaps as useless leather pants
That had the seat worn out. The parable
Is useless though unless you are aware
This was a good, hardworking hired man.

Between the Plattes the Lincoln Highway ran,
Concrete and smooth before the big trucks came;
Beside that ran the Union Pacific.
On both, one main street each, were wooden towns.
We knew them all but claimed the one nearby
Hometown by convenience of address.
Ours had a theater, two grocery stores
And a saloon, a post office and bank,
Three churches, two barbershops, a drugstore,
Shoe shop, hardware, blacksmith shop, garages,
Even a doctor and a dentist once,
A mortuary, a weekly newspaper,
And it claimed about six hundred people.
Times change, we say. The last time I was there,
Except for one bank, two churches (brick),
About all the inventory could show
Was one grocery store and two saloons.

But we became Southsiders later on
And turned our thoughts to lives of winter wheat
As well as lives of cows which we still kept
Among the sandhills farther to the north.
And then we turned to other things and left.

Before we're lost completely to the land,
Before the land leaves us, as we go now,
Its sound and sight and smell and speech and all
That formed our consciousness and consciences
And kept us up with what we really were
And kept us down to what we really are
Might form a song or two in celebration
Or make a metaphor for meditation.

I live again between the Plattes, upstream,
The water more transparent, it would seem:
More clarity the wish of every dream.

1862

These sandhills lie like balls of dung
Some giant scarabaeid flung,
Creating incubating piles
In rounded heaps for miles on miles
To pass beneath our wagon tongue.

Beside this trail the Platte runs clear
Though muddied somewhat east of here:
All the rest is brown or dun,
Bleached and shimmering in the sun.
We crawl along on running gear.

I'm sick of tumblebug ascents
And jolting days in schooner tents
And biting flies and alkali dust
And valleys walled with chalk rock crust
And all the shortgrass prairie scents.

But I suppose the men won't rest
With rolling all our hopes out west
To parch them in this horrid land;
They'll bury them in shifting sand
Like any scarabaeus nest.

Chimney Rock

The challenge was to be first to see Chimney Rock,
young twentieth century pioneers traveling west
by car (Plymouth), a challenge we took seriously,
being born along the Platte—Chimney Rock, most famous
of Oregon Trail landmarks. Even as children we knew
things like that. We knew of Plymouth Rock too,
though I'm sure we didn't make the connection then.
We were westerners traveling west to Grandma's house,
first to Bayard, until Grandpa two died, then to
Scottsbluff for Grandpa number three. (Grandpa number
one was long since gone. Grandma was a pioneer
in more ways than one.)

But pioneers we were in our imaginations, knew
Courthouse Rock and Jail Rock too, had seen
the paintings of covered wagons in the passes.
(My brother was always last to see these rocky,
formations: that's how we discovered he needed
glasses.) And always on the right ran the North River
as we called the North Platte, sometimes with small
flights of rapid mallards or lines of geese above.
It seems a little strange that even then we carried
in ourselves a profound sense of westering.
Perhaps it was because we used horses too, knew
cow chips burned like buffalo chips—we had burned
them—played "cowboys and Indians" on horseback,
knew our other grandpa had come west on a wagon,
trailed our cattle to the sandhills as in the old days
used the old ways, in country yet unchanged. At
night, at Easter Time, at the base of Chimney Rock,
we attended Passion Plays.

Those trips past Chimney Rock are vivid still. Now,
no longer young, my mind is often full of what
that westering on the Great Platte River Road must
have been: long days and hard work, dust and insects,
storms, uncertainty and danger, sweat and strain at
every hill—many days a test of will—so we've
been told. Yet, such a journey would itself fulfill,
one's need to move on to something new and better.
And hardship on the trail was not every traveler's lot:
diaries from those travelers have reports that read
like poetry: they don't always talk of hardship,
and the truth is most of them made it West just fine.
They were used to wagon travel in their time, and
horseback too. Indeed, death was no more common
on the trail than in the eastern cities and country
they left behind. The natives were in fact more help
than hindrance. Why we tend to romanticize their

journey in the negative says more of our soft lives
than the realities of their kind. Our pioneers had time
to carve their names on Chimney Rock, thousands of
them, though the names didn't last in the soft Brule clay,
and we can't see any of them today. Thirty years after
their great adventure, should they want to go East again
they could go down to the station and take a train.

In my imagination I travel with them
on the "Great Medicine Road," as the natives
were said to have named it, "buffler" beyond counting,
acres of prairie grouse, herds of pronghorn, and elk;
and air so clear that from to top of Scott's bluff you
can see Laramie Peak in Wyoming. I would see
the great Columbia as a river, and Celilo Falls.
I am familiar with many details already, having
grown up to the sound and smell of animals,
the creak of harness and saddle leather, know of
wooden wheels and running gear, know mixed grass
and short grass and dust, can drive a team or ride a
mustang, if I must. I'm familiar with grasshoppers,
sweat bees, nose flies, and gnats; I don't like them
but I can handle that. Wind I'm used to, hail and
lightning too. There would be no power lines or
wind machines to compromise the view; in the
distance everything would be clean and new. In my
mind it would be a great five-month adventure.

Indeed, I have traveled much of the route, pulled
by gas or pushed by diesel in my modern "Conestoga,"
followed the Platte across Nebraska, the Sweetwater up,
crossed South Pass, followed the Snake down, camped at
Farewell Bend, have been down the Columbia to
the ocean shore and back again. From Chimney Rock
to the present, there's a feeling I can't shake: put
simply, it seems I was born a hundred years too late.

Barbed Wire

At first there was no way to keep things out
And equally no way to keep things in—
The land refused to yield a barrier
So all that lived here mingled. Tumbleweed
And Model T's roamed freely over ground
Where once the bison migrated at will.
My father steered to dances by the stars.
How he got home I never heard him say.
Then came barbed wire and fence posts from the east,
Soon followed by the windmill, by the way—
Machines filling in gaps that nature left
When she left out the trees and stones and springs.
Before the wire and windmill came the Colt,
I've heard somewhere: neat manmade trinity
to subdue the prairie.
                                    Well, anyway
The means to keep things out and in arrived
To put a rapid end to any doubt
About whose place was whose in pointed fact
Though there are those who still profess to see
That barbs on every fence must point both ways.
A tumbleweed of any decent size
Gets stopped before it tumbles very far
Providing music of a wailing kind

When wind wails through it held against the wire.
It's nice that birds now have a place to perch
Though meadowlarks prefer to use the posts,
And frequently you see a singing bird
Above a singing wire. It's hard to say
If fences of barbed wire are aids to song
Or loud, thorny crowns a million miles long.

Windmills

Gray, galvanized metal petals
Balance on a derrick stalk,
Whine with wind-spin
Drive steel rod in
Rasp the casing, make it squawk.

Wild wind shifting slaps the tail fin,
Forces swinging where it's pinned,
Turns the vanes out
Fills the pipe spout—
Windmills face into the wind.

Hunting Arrowheads

Blowouts are the spots to hunt
For arrowheads. The ground is bare
And sand lies clean in rippled waves,
Except for a tenacious runt
Of soapweed growing here or there,
Exposing roots like barrel staves.

Go the day after a wind,
A wild wind that blows the sand
Under your collar. Windy days
Sift sand wherever grass is thinned;
But blowouts—being barren land—
The wild days blow their tops away,

Exposing anything that's there.
Remember now: days that are rough
Do groundwork that's essential here.
Then pick your spot and hunt with care—
You never will take care enough—
And keep your eye on ground quite near.

No way of telling what you'll find—
Scraper, bird point—pottery piece
Sometimes. All those people dead—
Think of it—leaving flint behind
Where lives were led, each sandy crease
A coffin marked with arrowhead.

Buffalo Skull

(Hear the drum?)

I found a skull
In buffalo grass—
A buffalo skull
With holes for eyes
Where long sand grass
Had filled each eye;
Its horns were dull
And gray, not black.
The skull faced east
In thanks to gods
Who furnished meat
Which made life good.
I wonder, hunter—
Who faced the east
And turned this skull
To face the sun
To thank the gods—
How you wondered
To see those gods
Who from that sun
Have come.

1959

The blizzard left the hilltops bare
But filled the low spots everywhere.
Snowdrift shrouds blocked all the roads;
Feeding took two extra loads
Of hay and cake, and extra care.

So when I heard the news at ten—
The wind was down, the sun bright then,
Usual weather after a storm—
I went to get the engine warm
And search the hills with other men.

Ten minutes up I found her car.
She hadn't driven very far
Before she stalled below a hill
Three miles beyond her school windmill
Where summer desert roses are.

I landed on a wind-cleared rise
So small it took me several tries
And found she had two tires flat.
You can't go far in snow like that.
She stared at me through frozen eyes.

I can't say now just how I felt.
Blizzards are things with which I've dealt—
I've seen their snows blow white as death
To blind the eyes and choke off breath,
And then in two days gently melt.

Branding

Bawling anger
Pain white eyes
Smoking stench of flaming hair,
Living leather
Squeaks its cries
Accepts the scar that's branded there.

Red-hot sears right,
Sunset red,
Searing brands on yearling skin;
White-hot, too hot
Cuts instead
Leaves a wound where flies get in.

Burning sharply
Branding well
Never push hot irons much:
Smears are ugly;
Brands all tell
Marking takes a special touch.

Middleground

In memory of my mother

I know a house that stands between
A pasture and a field of wheat
As if attempting to equate
A legend with a present feat,
As if to understand old grass
Were to explain the new machines
Or justify a backward past
By reference to present means.

The woman of this house I've seen
Has planted plum and cherry trees
And other plants that she can raise
Against a hostile prairie breeze.
When winter comes she leaves the yard
And fills the porch with potted bloom
So keeps herself from being scarred
By fate and too much living room.

Man

I've seen the desert roses bloom
Where cactus wouldn't grow,
Where all they had was living room
And moisture from the snow;
And yet it's fairly hard to find
A petal shade more rare—
Just like the color or my mind
Since you've been blooming there.

Woman

Your voice if like the voice of doom—
You speak to all I know—
I have to blame the gibbous moon,
Which makes my nature show.
But that which moves us is unkind
In tempting us to share
In what we have to leave behind
In time, regardless of our care.

Rattlesnake

The design of the snake—
That elongated shape—
Has suggested to some
The wrong kind of fun,
Reminder of pleasure
So worthy of censure.
Pleasure becomes then
An extension to sin,
And with hardly a breath
Sin extends on to death.

Our rattler has stature,
Considered for pleasure:
He holds his tail erect
In order to protect
The rattles at the end.
You quickly apprehend
The erection herein
Which refers to the sin.
But what of the rattles?
For amorous battles?

Aren't these rattles maybe
Intended for baby?
An obvious banner
In rattlesnake manner
Suggesting fruition
In nature's tradition?
Perhaps the snake has fed

On some small quadruped
And that bulging you see
Promises pregnancy.

At least it seems unfair
To leave suggestion where
Those older stories do,
Arbitrarily choose
To confuse creation
With plain procreation.
But though we've banished sin
Which is quickly done when
We give the picture breadth
We're still faced with death.

For death the rattler deals.
His concern is the real.
He hunts throughout the night
His intention to strike;
And he will find his mark
Sensing life in the dark.
At the end of the role
He swallows his prey, whole.
His belly is replete;
We see him now complete.

It might be hard to take
A common rattlesnake
For what he's always been—
Not much concerned with sin.
Nor was he ever bred
With remorse for the dead.
Leave him there distended;
Nature so intended:
For few have it in them
To deal with such venom.

Getting the Point

With most prairie plants I find
Nature seems defensive.
Then I bump a growing spine;
It seems offensive.

Yucca, cactus, puncture-weed
And one we call sticker
Are a prickly sounding breed
To any thinker.

Doesn't knowing what plants are
In a pasture make it
Not so much the way things are
As how we take it?

Coyote

Pencil muzzle
Pyramidal ears
Slim gray body
Jaw that tears
Small round footprint
Long bush tail
Super hearing
Eyes yellow, pale
Crafty, cunning
Hard to trap
Prairie winds howl
And he howls back.

Pronghorn

(*Antilocapra americana*)

Not wholly goat
Nor antelope
Is his written
Negative description.
Why compare
This creature here
With creatures where
There's too much goat
Too little antelope?
But we'll accept
The mean in that
If, as we hope,
It means more antelope
Than goat.

Yet for himself
He is unique:
Of runners he's most fleet.
Each year
He drops
His special horn—
Both prong
And point
By nature shorn—
What's more,
He sheds the sheath
But keeps the core

Then grows
The point
And prong
Once more.
And he wears
Erectile hairs,
Heliograph bump
Upon his rump.
His decision
Depends on
Telescopic vision.
He is
Well adapted
Though neither goat
Nor antelope
The American born
Pronghorn.

Winter Wheat

Planted near the fall, in dry September
In dark earth beside stiff, bleaching stubble
Seeds with Indian names, Cheyenne, Pawnee,
Green against the snows of late November.
It is perhaps that soil enriched by drought
Is suited to this grain that's planted late
And grows best against the grain of winter.
Holding hardily through December's wind
Nipped close and bruised by grazing animals
It stools to lushness on a frozen ground;
And with the thaws of spring it springs to heights
That ripple with the wind, to waves of spears
With frosted beards, rows of swelling kernels.
Winter tested seed makes summer harvests.

Flower

A camera made the image of the flower;
A computer enlarged it greatly.
What showed was not some fairy bower
Found in children's stories lately.

There, crouched in hairs and glinting eyes,
A black spider eyed its tiny prey:
A green leaf hopper less than half its size
Poised for an attempt to get away.

What the outcome was we'll never know;
The instant image froze the scene.
We can assume if we could watch the show
An outcome proper to a lurid dream.

Meadowlark

Earliest spring singer
And last to be heard in the fall
The immodest meadowlark
Swells with the worth of it all.

From his fencepost pulpit
Or, lacking a fence, from the ground
He proclaims that everything's right.
He's right, if you judge by sound.

Assurance he delivers
Without ever missing a word;
The way he straightens his shoulders
Who'd guess that he's just blackbird.

Such cheerful rectitude
Would suggest it's improper to seek
Whether he really makes music
Or just runs off at the beak.

As birds go he's common,
With his urgent desire to nest;
Just a needle nosed singer
Outside, with egg on his vest.

Lark Bunting

May male buntings fly into the sun
Then sing their mating songs in swoops,
Each swoop a different sound
Much closer to the ground—
A reluctant descendentalism,
An unhawk-like stoop
With a lilt ending each one—
As many as six separate swoops
For six separate songs sung
At night as well as daylong
By a small, black, bird flashing white shoulders
Over a bright prairie and a small, dull
Dun bird waiting on the ground.
And I have heard the sounds
All night filling the air for all its worth
And have to admire a bird who can sing his songs
While coming down to earth.

Horned Larks

Most numerous of birds and most unlarklike
Ground hugging horned larks appear—
Wherever short grass grows
Circumpolar the northern globe
In quick flocks of feathered chaff
Or weakly cheeping sunlit sparks
At any disturbance—and disappear.
But they're always here.
Blizzard or drought, tame and unmusical
With horns as soft as their voices
Ubiquitous in modesty
Constant as the low humidity
Dependable as the dust
Predictable in glancing flights
They show themselves,
Like love.

Windy Gap

My immediate family began in Windy Gap,
A steep, sandy pass through the rugged sandhills
That separate the North Platte from the South Platte.

At least according to family talk (tradition?)
My father proposed to my mother there.
I came very respectably later (in the Depression).

A Windy Gap setting has always been good for a pun.
I still can't tell whether it's simply the effect of the past,
But that cut through the hills was consistently given to fun.

For example, a favorite story my uncles liked to tell
Was of backing over the pass with the girls at night
To gravity feed gas to the motor when gas was *short as hell.*

But to get back to my earlier, stern intention—
Which was to capitalize upon this metaphorical luck
And, incidentally, conquer doggerel with invention—

Or maybe just keep sanity safe in flippancy
By not paying strict attention to the suspicion
That one is about to touch a macabre consistency.

Whatever—a metaphor is like a proposal—
We're stuck with the result, and that's the trouble.
We have but one set of handy myths at our disposal.

One wonders if there in the gap the proposal was windy
And if they stopped romantically at the height of the pass.
Probably they said and acted out whatever was handy.

They did the acceptable thing, handled the situation,
Managed the problem of being two separate sexes
By agreeing to participate in the standard solution.

Their reward was not immediately obvious:
It began with my coming, and others followed;
That all of us were deliberate is rather dubious

Unless one really believes in deliberate poverty
Or deliberate ignorance. Chances are, like most,
They took for granted the limitations of family

Or didn't notice what they traded for what they got.
It's very unpopular yet to poke fun at family—
Anyone's family, the idea of family, or anyone so begot.

Maybe they never considered themselves in a trap,
Or knew they transcended a dirty joke with acceptance,
Or cared my own beginning began in Windy Gap.

Crop Failure

A normal year—
Summer's rain on time
September's planting quickly done
Winter's moisture fine
Spring's winds hurt little
Even on the hills;
Later things that ruin grain
The common ills:
Black rust from too much cloudiness
Red rust from too much rain
Aphids, "Hessian fly," too hot a breeze
Too cool a rain—
Nothing happened
Enough to spoil a crop.
I expected grain.

One normal cloud
Came with the evening sun
In time to douse the normal pink—
I saw the lightning come,
Knew long before the light had failed
My crop was hailed.

First Son

Different he was to some.
Old before his time, he'd come
Already weaned it seemed—
Made ironical. He dreamed
Alone on Saturday nights
Worried over others' fights
His only fight a bully
Never defeated fully—
He never had enough size.
Yet any slight got a rise
Out of him before he learned
To put (this much he had learned)
A damper on his temper.
But, truth to say, his anger
Appeared to be directed
At something he'd detected
In the way things had been made.
He himself seemed unafraid
Of anything that got said
About where his future led
Because he would not respect
Or take time to protect
Our normal, local customs.

What were some local customs?
One custom was ambition;
Another was contrition.
To point out contradiction
Was my first son's affliction.

Another short example:
Horse lovers like to trample
People, he said he'd noticed.
He claimed to find small solace
In "healthy competition":
He harbored a suspicion
That that's what winners called it.

Because some art requires wit
Entertain with tragedy
(Murder makes the mystery),
Drama often got too close
(Tragedy too large a dose).
He always avoided those
Even in the picture shows.
I'm not in this culture bit
Much myself of course, but it
Does seem that his reminder
That the world could be kinder
Fits my own experience—
After all there is the sense
Real life is hard enough.

He himself was country tough,
Meaning hard work and long days
Had already established ways
To a personal regard
Found in those who find it hard
To agree with what's thought common
Sense. *That's what makes it common,*
He liked to say. He was young
Yet too, of course, and among
His many interests were
Books, music, girls and laughter;
He played ball, went to dances
Sang in church, took his chances

With our horses in the hills,
Which, incidentally, filled
Some need for being outside
Alone.

It's doubtful he felt profound;
Maybe he'd already found
It's harder to tell what's real
Than fabricate an ideal,
Like the time love was the thing—
Real, he thought. He could not bring
His own sensibility
Into the vicinity
Of simple lust—understand
That what he conceived as grand
Was probably too ideal
For normal folks to feel—
That finding excuse to breed
Was all he'd ever need—
Here I'm being cynical
Where he would be sensible
(Too sensible to try rhyme
In odd couplets anytime).

I suppose I'm not alone
In having to claim my own.

Scattered Thunderstorms

It seems we're always looking up,
Late afternoon and evening.
It may be we should wonder why,
For clouds can be deceiving.

We live on land called semi-arid,
Arid too, in some locations.
We view the sky, it must be said,
With mixed anticipations.

We're always in need of moisture;
Most comes from winter snow.
The rest must arrive in summer,
Or not all that we plant will grow.

We can use a gentle rainfall;
We look forward to gentle rain.
But thunderstorm wind can ruin all—
Lay waste a whole field of grain.

And we don't need a lightning bolt
That fires a field or pasture,
Or kills a mare and newborn colt—
All we need is moisture.

And hail is not unusual—
Destroyer flung from the sky.
These storms are never casual—
Sometimes we'd prefer to be dry.

The irony here should be patent:
We look to the storms for rain;
But their dangers are well beyond latent;
We often lose more than we gain.

Some among us like to pretend
That's nature's way must be good.
It might be so for you my friend—
It's not always so in my neighborhood.

Clarification

I wouldn't be here
In the rodeo bleachers
If I thought the performance
Consisted of preachers.
Sometimes when I go
To the rodeo grounds
I sit way up high
And just watch the clowns.

(Note: in the rodeo arena, men dressed as clowns protect the participants from being physically harmed by the animals. The clowns often protect themselves by jumping into large padded wooden or steel barrels.)

Burrowing Owl

Mild, unblinking observer,
Wide-eyed assessor
Of prairie dog towns,
Most often observed as himself
In large yellow eyes
Just above ground,
Or peering in pairs
From the shelf
Of a quick formal bow
On a mound
Near a prairie dog burrow
He borrowed,
Is the non-burrowing
Burrowing owl.

Old Timer

These once silent spaces are loud with sound;
Murmur of grasses is lost to the plow;
Men who craved silence all mold in the ground.

The whine of high engines keeps shouting down
Protests of human integrity now—
These once silent spaces are loud with sound.

Offspring of screaming view with a frown
That silent outcast whose strangeness warns how
Men who craved silence all mold in the ground.

The voice of the coyote sells by the pound
As all buyers hear the voice of the cow:
These once silent spaces are loud with sound.

Auctioneer peoples begin to surround
Each other with ever increasing row.
Men who craved silence all mould in the ground

And noisy, glassed canyons nowadays abound—
Elegant witness to man's furrowed brow—
These once silent spaces are loud with sound;
Men, who craved silence, all mold in the ground.

Feeling the Wind

In memory of Kodo Lightfoot

Always there in bending grasses
Moaning yuccas, singing fences
Blowing wind in prairie places,
Feel it softly on your cheek
Know I'm there—my way to speak
When I am gone. Already weak
I tell you now before I'm dead.
That's the Apache way, she said.
Feeling now the winds' caresses
Something more than country zephyrs
I keep listening to the breezes
Hoping there to hear her speeches,
Wishing now my words might share
A sigh with hers in keening air.

"Relations"

Relatives are "relations" where I grew up;
parents, aunts, and uncles numbered twenty-one,
cousins beyond counting, at least by me, not one
to keep track of a family tree. All stayed with the land
except three or four. My father's brothers were Fred,
John, Henry, Pete, and Harry. His sisters were Katherine
Anna, Dorothy, and Helen. Mother's sisters were Esther and
Lydia.
Then all but one married, adding Roger and Andy,
Ray, Earl, and Louie, Marie and May, Emma and Elma—
only Fred did not carry the family farther: after army abroad,
he came back to farm with a brother, took care of his
mother, raised beets, "spuds" and cattle, corn and alfalfa.

Harry survived the South Pacific, his mission to drive
a landing craft to the beach, the pumps pumping blood
before he could reach sand. He managed to survive
to retirement at age sixty-five. A hospital infection ended him.
Now they're all gone except one—uncle by marriage,
Harry's wife's brother, who's now ninety-one—whose wife,
by the way, had been Harry's twin sister, gone recently.
I'm sure the others too had stories to tell, had I known
them as well. Country lives follow seasons, complicated
by weather as a matter of course: hardship happened,
but not a single divorce. The next generation (cousins by name),
although living better by far, can not make that claim.

Nothing then as dependable as family, for practical reasons
like help in the fields, or close private relationships
of mutual community, closely bound to earth in more
than one way, as those of the soil are "like to say."
Since the earth we inhabit holds more dead than alive,
I remember them here so, perhaps for a while, their names
might survive, not in verse "more sounding than bronze,"
(we're neither Roman nor Greek) but in us when we speak.

Hank

We called my uncle Henry "Hank."
My first memory has him constructing a boat
in my grandparents' house; he was working
in the dining room, a room of note for size
and family get-togethers. It was a big room
with a big table: it had to be for a farm family
of size, ten and the parents, and now able
to accommodate daughters-in law and sons,
grandchildren, toys, and country noise.
There he was, bending over wooden parts,
well-formed ribs and small brass screws,
the big table moved, as I recall, over to one side.
The boat had already taken shape, but
lacked its outer cover yet. Though still small
I was in awe: I knew what a boat was—but
in the house? In the dining room? At any rate,
that, I think, is my first memory of Uncle Hank.

Later encounters for me were few,
but I always knew Hank was the outdoor type.
He showed how his curly haired retrievers
could jump for a glove on top of a post,
though I never saw him use the boat.
Like all the rest he became a farmer,
was financed in part by my father, put up hay,
grew other crops near Brule's South River.
Much later I showed up early one morning to
look for deer. He answered the door unshaven
and showed me where. My father once had to

remind him it wasn't smart to drive a car with
hot exhaust through sandhill grass in summer.

Though he lived near a river, I don't think my
Uncle Henry ever knew things like another Henry
once lived on Walden; I could be wrong: it has been
reported to me that Henry, Jr. became an MD.
(Would fit my family's history.)

"Chewing the Fat"

Whenever we get together,
No matter by chance or design,
We always talk about weather,
Of interest all of the time.

Besides, without controversy,
It's easy for talk to begin:
All share in weather's perversity,
No matter if stranger or friend.

We all agree it's been too hot.
We all agree it's been too dry.
Wind's done more damage than we thought;
Knocked down too much wheat and some rye.

Rain's been too late for this and that,
Too soon for stacking wild, wet hay.
All this talk (called "chewing the fat")
Reminds us all of nature's way:

Some always prefer to pretend
That nature's plan is always good.
(Unless there's been some helpful trend,
It's not so in my neighborhood.)

Chewing the fat often moves on,
Weather having broken the ice,
To things that interest everyone
Business, family, suffice.

Religion, politics, are taboo,
Unless, of course, we all agree—
Then we may talk of something new,
And one might hear, *I see, I see.*

Town and Country

One must have been born in the city or town
To find anything urban worth putting down:
That has been true for me most of the time—
Country things only invested with rhyme.

Exceptions have been casual rehearsal,
Slighting some themes and truths universal.
Yet since I've spent much of my life in the city;
I suppose I deserve some suburban pity.

Dirt

I present to you
Dirt, capital **D**.
I demand that everyone see
its absolute indispensability—
praise those involved in its husbandry.

From carrots to cotton, rice to wheat,
the grasses that feed our sources of meat,
from beets to hops (and alcohol neat)
the caretakers of dirt from each county seat
bring life to us all, and then they repeat.

What's more I assert
that those of the soil are much more alert
to all basic truth—earth's laws made overt—
for the rest of us too that it wouldn't hurt
to measure what's real through the lessons of dirt.

Formal Sitting

In memory of my father

No. Snap the shutter while I steer
this combine here through ripened wheat.
I don't care to pose.

Expose your film in blizzard light,
while I break through knee-deep drifts,
find a wet new calf, calm its fright,
wrap it in burlap, slap it's flanks,
lay it near the kitchen stove.

Snap a shot while the iron's hot
burning my "O-Bar" brand;
make a view of the castrating knife—
blood on my hand.

Don't worry scenes that can't be caught.
I'll not pretend to what I'm not.
And I expect you'll understand.

Hills and Valleys

Last night in the forties
I shivered mosquitoes
Today in the nineties
Swat flies in the dust—
Last week I rode green hills
Last month slipped in sleeting,
Without wind for windmills
Remember snow drifting—
Sometimes from my dreaming
I wake up still trying
To keep myself even
In living and dying.

Autumn Walk

Quo vadis? I thought, strolling cheerfully,
Watching the parallel hurry on Main;
Could so many be arriving tardily
At such pressing business someplace in the van?
Quo vadis traffici? might be appropriate—
Yet, considering the strength of the thing,
Payments and other forced pace in environment,
Quo vadis Domine? had the right ring.

Well, my measure would still be humanity,
Sharp autumn wind met with feet and with mind;
I know how mechanical mobility
Pretends an importance that leaves me behind.
Then I heard mind, with soft, mocking laughter
Inform me I was walking faster.

Autumn Talk

Autumn trim skirts and shiny hair—
I know your little girl, said one;
The other smiled. What do you do?
We talked. They walked me toward their school.
Can you cross without the patrol boy?
We have to wait for the patrol boy—
But we can cross with you;
We can cross with teachers and grownups.

We crossed together. There was no real traffic.
They could have crossed alone. Thank you, they said.
So I resumed my normal pace
And watched them join the playground crowd
And had the time to wonder how
I'd manage by myself just now.

Poem for Jill

(occasional)

Some birthdays are special,
not for the count, but for the care taken
just getting there—
as this is with Jill, daughter so smart
she can so handle tough going
that might break your heart.
She does things so well
we are filled with respect
that along with our love
makes this the best birthday
yet.

Recognition

So strange seems this hand
That reached for the wine
Wrinkled and freckled
From too much sunshine—
Knuckles like ridges,
Thick fingers through time,
Thin skinned, age spotted—
How could it be mine?

And what of this face
That peers from the glass
With crows' feet showing
And whitened moustache—
Thin hair, high forehead
In place of black thatch—
Face in reflection
The hand's marks can match?

And what of the thinking
Improved by the wine
Warmed by the liquor
And passing of time?
Old times remembered,
Remembered lifetime,
Distant adventures—
Might those have been mine?

For Delia, Her Poems

Gifted beyond words
How could I tell you then
Or now finally of all persons
How brave I heard you
Who would have understood
Whose brave it was my daughter
That taught me courage?
And who will will me patience now?
Given ordinary wisdom
We might have sung our songs together
With ordinary days for laughter
Before you had to pen
Your metaphor forever.

I'll See You Still in Every Living Thing

I'll see you still in every living thing
And know you'll occupy my heart somehow
When I no longer have new songs to sing.

Chrysanthemums will bloom and fall birds sing
Spring buds will burst on every laurel bough—
I'll see you still in every living thing.

Lark buntings make their music on the wing.
Black-headed searching gulls will find the plow
When I no longer have new songs to sing.

The dappled fawn was always born to bring
Such innocence as nature will allow.
I'll see you still in every living thing.

New life will gambol free with every spring,
Colts with mares, piglets with a mother sow
When I no longer have new songs to sing.

Though children's play makes valleys ring
Paternal care now wears a troubled brow:
I'll see you still in every living thing
When I no longer have new songs to sing.

Autobiography

To know me you would have to hear
My mother's singing in the kitchen,
Touch my father's leather winter mittens.
You'd have to know my wife's grave silences,
My daughters' happy prattle when we drove—
You'd know a tiny schnauzer's tilted muzzle
Meant she knew the gist of every word.

You'd understand which mood means rhyme,
Which topic lends itself to plain blank verse.
You'd understand how teal tell time—
At least in terms of spring and fall—
Know sounds of mallard wings at twilight,
Dawn's modest whickered greeting from a stall.

You'd need to know defining moments—
Private assessments of things best kept
Unspoken, unhinted, silent, unwept—
Know there are those, foreign as termites
Living deep within secluded ground—
Where only in a fatal light's exposure
Might one discover everything profound.

Thune

Dun and fading
Like the murmur of an ancient rune
An aging reminiscence
Pictures Thune:
Dun and fading landscape
Wooden sandhill town,
One store behind one gas pump
Long ago torn down—

I think it was the post office near Flats.

I see it at the turning
Of the rolling, sandy track,
But even if I wanted to
I know I can't get back.

Can't get back to Thune—
Would violate some natural law,
And so becomes the desert space
That is my ultima . . .

Prairie Sunflowers

(Helianthus petiolaris)

It's September now, and prairie roads bloom yellow once again.
Ragged, disordered, bristly stalks rear up above all other growth,
decorate the plain. Complex heads of ray, disk, and counter whorls
turn daily with the sun—dawn to dusk. We understand: when
summer's done we follow light—north to south, not east to west—
turn our heads toward southern warmth in concert with the sun.

We're told the native prairie folk made medicine and food of them,
and pigment too for decoration, even planted some for larger seed
in careful plant selection. Newer plants through countless years
have added to the seeds' dimensions. Now we drive by hybrid fields,
single blooms large as platters, food for birds and humans too,
like spitting baseball batters. We prefer the roadside plants, in cheerful
awkward, random stems, countless blooms, and independent patterns.

We're glad to see these complex blooms—two flowers making one—
jealous plants, roots warding off the competition. We're also sad
to see them come so promptly to fruition—our reason?—their color
is a certain sign we too again will follow sun, leave far behind
these flowers of a fading season—in our own fading season.

Upstream

It's drier now, more rugged too;
High desert can be sere and mean.
I guess I'll learn to see it through—
Though lonely since I moved upstream.
The cactus here outgrows the grass;
Most moisture comes from melting snow.
I miss my shortgrass prairie past
And those who taught me what I know.
I know nothing's made to last—
Can't get it back, can't let it go.

Mountain

Saturday Morning

Westerly's up a bit this morning, ruffling
magazine pages as I park myself on Lakehouse's
redwood now gray deck, somehow strangely content
though blocked from lake view by a neighbor's
new boat, pondering the containing of ephemeral
mood in unspoken words, written words, that is,
phonemes and morphemes the real sounds of meaning,
symbols on a page infinitely inadequate, wondering
at the morning's necessity to make sense of unspoken
words to a contentment I do not deserve, being
lately told I'm already old, too late to be discovered
until too late, like Emily.

I think, perhaps, I'll just let this mood compose
itself within my head, without any active participation
instead of trying to control the moment anyway,
having learned by now that procrastination is a
virtue, just dismiss the mirror, youthful indifference
and deference too, enjoy the unexpected view of
myself painless in body and mind for awhile, able to
smile at myself the brief egoist, or at least, so I hope,
here alone on the redwood now gray deck, inhaling
a cool morning air, rocking a little in our old deck
chair, pondering the source of an uncommon mood
on a Saturday morning.

Time

When I retire for the night,
I take off time
and lay it on the dresser—
not the same as in the light
I take time off, a lesser
version, but in either case
it will be there when
I want to pick it up again.
Of course I am aware
that though I take care
when I lay it down
it yet might not be there
if pilfered by the unknown.

Dream

I was trying to climb steep, too steep,
make-do slippery, yellow sandy steps
to a make-do weekend cabin,
being told it was mine. It wasn't.
I gave up the climb but found a door
to rooms too cluttered to be pleasant—
full of collections: on the right, bookcases
with complete series of audio books
of popular fiction, the kind of make-believe
I haven't time for, even in dreams it seems;
on the left, in my way, two long tables
covered with dozens of musty, rusty vises.

On the high sand bank I followed the line
looking for mine among the varied places.
It wasn't there, not even close, but building
was going on: wire and boards, and other—
and near the end, among some braided wire,
picking up some wire was my father,
neither old nor dead, looking slim and fit,
smiling faintly. Surprised, I said, *Hi Dad,*
and woke up sad. That was it.

Grand Tetons

French trappers were obviously
earthy enough, normal males in their prime
naming, perhaps, these instant peaks
for Indian wives of that time:
mountains without foothills rising full-peaked
from sagebrush plains through snow line.

I have seen them change with the seasons,
sunlight descend with the coming day,
remember them clouded and in clear air,
especially when I've been away.
I never wanted to mount them;
I just like knowing they're there.

Damselfly Days

Rains ended last night.
Against clearing sky,
In mid-June daylight
I see damselflies fly.
See more than one—
Until numbers fade—
Too hot in the sun,
Too cool in the shade.

Fiery Narrows

(4th of July, 2009, Alcova Lake, Wyoming)

The flags are out on every place, and not this time only
to let you know the weekend crowd and permanent
summer residents are here: today the country's birthday
is in the air, here, where Fremont the Pathfinder found a path
along the Platte that wrecked his boat but wrote a diary note
naming narrow places with towering red cliffs along the route.
"Fiery Narrows" he called them, and we are near.
Occasionally we hear clandestine fireworks. Every place
with space to camp along the lake is taken—few tents,
many travel trailers, campers, motorhomes ("RV's"),
boats nearby, "jet skis," and other water toys. We are not
a poor people, despite the sanctimonious pity sniffled
from the current national news. Most of us are working.
The surface of the lake is shaken by traffic, power or sail;
streets have chairs in place to claim scarce parking space.

We're here to celebrate our founding, and other places
of our early history are nearby—Independence Rock,
of an earlier 4th of July is just upstream, the names
of early pioneers still visible to the naked eye, reminder
on the Sweetwater near where it joins the Platte of
dogged westering on the trail to "where rolls the Oregon,"
with Cate's and Martin's coves of Mormon pushcart
tragedy almost in view. (A visitors' center there is nearly new.)
We are familiar with our nation's early roaming: after all,
we are of Wyoming. We take for granted space for
personal mobility, an active kind of freedom,
are suspicious of restrictions, keep the Second Amendment

well in mind and visible too, know that remaining free
requires a well-armed citizenry, have little use for any
who might think differently. Some of us, many perhaps,
have in uniform followed the red, white, and blue,
spent some personal capital for liberty.

Here in the land of the prudent we have the witless too,
leaving their spoor as cans from brew near roads, on streets,
in borrow pits, requiring sheriffs deputies' vehicles
in view. Such celebrants are indifferent to the 4th itself,
birth of a new country, unique social arrangement;
or death on the 4th of July of two of its original creators,
founders John Adams and Thomas Jefferson. Others of us
remember them and through them freedom's price. We
celebrate them also; and remember James Monroe, another
of our founders who died on the 4th as well. His place in
memory is forever secure, and his "Doctrine" is right still.
For the present, sometimes we hear sirens, and Life Flight
sits padded near the boat club just in case.

Mainly, its a time for families to celebrate together;
license plates from other states show up. The ages mingle:
grandparents reminisce; babies cry, teenagers roam
the streets in pairs or groups, never single, or ride the tailgates
of pickups, jet skis, or boats; couples hold hands or leashes
as dogs pull them along. The smoke and scent of barbeque
is everywhere accompanied by laughter, and after lunch
(dinner) or dinner (supper) everyone complains that he or she
ate too much. We are a mixed lot, but we respect each other.
Make no mistake: we can distinguish between the genuine
and the fake or false. We all share work and loss. It's a hard
land: we make jokes of our two seasons, winter and almost winter.
Today, on the 4th of July, we wear sweaters and jackets
against cold rain. We hope it won't snow on the 4th again.

Before dark an impromptu parade forms, no floats—just an
almost real calliope, some flag waving resident marchers,
some small children with decorated bicycles, riding or prancing
through a cheering, clapping gantlet of applause—after dark
sometimes, before the fireworks over the lake, a lighted parade
of boats, horns blowing.

We have been told the Life Flight helicopter is checking
the weather report: there have been daily thunderstorms
for weeks; and if a storm is coming, it will leave. It leaves.
We wait—families on the decks of cabins, in summer houses,
mobile homes, campers on the shore, boats on the lake.
Storm or no storm, we intend to celebrate. We intend to
recapitulate the rockets red glare, the bombs bursting in air.

The first rocket comes with the thunder. Our celebration
is a wonder—jagged lightning cracks behind bursting
rockets; the thunder thunders in tune to the rocket explosions
and flashing lights—and it all reverberates again and again
against the cliffs of Fiery Narrows. Rain comes. No matter.
The whistling of ascending ordinance, boom of flashing rocket
patterns accelerates. We have a fiery fireworks like no other in
our Fiery Narrows—unique, violent and full of fury,
but mostly ordered, generally in control—like ourselves,
like us, Wyoming citizens of "lands, lots of land
under starry skies above"—we take our clichés seriously—
"don't tread on me"—especially if they're part of history.
We "carry"—and those rifles in our pickup racks can be used
for more than venery. "Gun control" means hold steady and
fire carefully. We celebrate the 4th of July and liberty.
Only the effete, ignorant, and condescending think
we inhabit "fly over" country. We aim to care for freedom
and family. We are not citizens of the world: the USA
will do for us. Intrusive government is an abomination.
We vote. We're citizens of Wyoming and this nation.

Collared Dove

I know: Eurasian collared dove is your full name.
Like all of us, citizened now, familiar, you came
from somewhere far away. I hear your constant calling
every day, sounding lost and missing something. I can say
I sympathize somehow, feeling pretty lost myself
in a land of hyphenated citizenry. Perhaps, you will belong
more readily, helped by your constant song; we have
already begun to drop "Eurasian" from your name:
you have become that "collared dove" or (it's a shame)
that strange looking dove without a name that has that
squared-off white tail, pretty when extended.

There are those who have reacted with the usual line,
that you might be potential danger to doves already here.
So far, you seem to coexist just fine. I see you everywhere—
and hear your call. Certainly, not all who have imported
themselves or been imported here have added to our well-being—
starlings and cheat grass come to mind. I'm sure that
for a time they were hyphenated too. For myself,
I'm glad to have you here, one who stays to make a home,
not even flying to some southern country to winter,
as do a number of our part-time natives. At any rate,
I doubt your foreign origin will cling a hyphen for
three hundred years or more, or that your song will be
heard to slander what you came here for.

Wings

Tiny mood breaker buzzes for nectar
or soft curving beak coos from the ground
or declaims from tree tops, hops, flits,
soars, swoops, suspends upside down—
no matter my mood, light, serious,
dark, brooding, these flashes of
feathers or colors or singing
improve any morning,
reminding me wings
connect me to things.

Mountain Blue Bird

Blue as a Rocky Mountain sky
He flashed across the road,
But what really caught my eye
Was the intensity he showed.

He pursued some beige-winged prey:
I saw its wings flash in the sun.
He wouldn't let it get away;
He persisted and he won.

Irony flew in blue before me—
Beauty on the hunt to eat—
Aggression as necessity.
The lesson was complete.

Finch Feeders

We hang finch feeders north and south—
Made for inverted eaters only,
Ruse to flee from bored or lonely
At both north and southern house.

Goldfinches peck at summer thistle
(Named "American") in the guide.
"Lessers"—in winter where we reside—
Show among the thrasher's whistle.

House finches come to join the show,
Though not bred to feed head down,
Some learn to swing around
And snatch a seed or feed below.

But north or south these tiny creatures
Male, female, alone or paired
Practice constant fluttered warfare—
Pecking order in their natures.

Warfare here among the lowly,
Will this nature never stop?
There's a thought: most likely not.
We come to understanding slowly.

Fisherman

After wading until my back is tired,
legs a little shaky from water pressure
and rounded rubble, I stumble to the bank,
if there is one high enough for comfort,
to sit and smell the pine and fir, listen
to the river purr and gurgle, splash
in its dash to the Atlantic or Pacific,
eventually, far away, specific only when
I am thinking of the water I momentarily
live by. I may straighten or rebuild a leader;
I may tie on a new fly, mocking those nearby—
"matching the hatch."

Of feathers, fur, and tinsel, and a hundred
other materials, common, local, maybe
ornamental—there are thousands of patterns
made to match insects trout like: I choose
from those, or from those of my own
matching imagination, called dry, wet,
or in-between, depending on their use,
in or on the water: Royal Wulff, Coachman,
Trueblood Nymph—titles from fishers or
traditions of an older time. I sit on the bank
and participate in a well-worn tradition,
ancient mission, another kind of venery.

I am here only. I am alone but not lonely.
I am not a fisher of men: I am
a fisher of fish. I am most happy then,

content in the possible fruits of my own
skill, without doubt living for awhile
in a kind of self-imposed exile, selfish
perhaps (no pun intended), lost for a time
in time only mine. If I see a fish rise,
I will rise to the occasion, with rod
of oriental bamboo perhaps and reel
one might still find in the British Isles—
both far distant in more than miles.

Or I may fish from a boat—cruiser
or canoe, to power or float over fathoms
or shallows. I drift with the seasons,
watch mergansers and grebes, cast with ease
over shoals, troll languidly through waves,
crab with the wind. I keep busy with tackle:
untangle the lures, mend a net or a leader,
oil a reel, retie a snap, send another line out.
Or I laze in the sun behind wheel or tiller.
I like boats; I like water. I fish for all kinds—
whatever is there—I don't always care,
but sometimes admit to being selective a bit.

I have fished both oceans, the Gulf as well,
sounds, streams, and bays in Alaska too,
sometimes alone, sometimes with crew,
shared time with puffins, kittiwakes, gulls,
ospreys, and kites, heard dippers warble
beside rushing water. I don't fish all weathers:
I'm not there to improve my manhood or mood,
brag of success, by size, location, or number.
For a time I become merely part of the scene—
part of a world we call natural—I wander
in wonder, not thinking, just taking it in—
content for at time in the land of gullet and fin.

Lake or river, pond or stream, I never dream
of being elsewhere when I'm there. I feel
more there—there—if you know what I mean.
I am not so far from the cave as not to miss
the joys of my own harvesting when I
am elsewhere, deferential to someone else's
time, which is, of course, usually most of it.
At times, indeed, I catch a fish or two—or more.
I may put them back; I may take them ashore.
I don't fish to philosophize, apologize,
rationalize, or justify a sensitive humanity.
I fish for fish here, not on the Sea of Galilee.

Hunter

I've gone on hunts a million years—
(I speak now representing peers):
Propensity (for some the need),
Since we descended from the trees
To take the field in search of prey,
Now thought by some to be passé.
But what seems fortunate to me—
I was born with means to see
All of us for what we are:
I view "civilization" from afar.

My membership in fang and claw
Is completely natural after all,
I am complete in the out-of-doors;
Companion to all those on all fours
No better and no worse than they
Not guaranteed a better way
To come to nature's common end.
One difference: I can apprehend.
Another? I know nature's force
Means we all share a common source.

Of similarities there is another:
All species tend to hunt each other,
Though my own species does it more,
A different hunt, we call it war.
Unlike my quest war has no season
But my own kind find a reason
To carry on this endless passion

Peace itself quite out of fashion.
But I digress, I guess. I must explain
A paradox in language plain:

For first—a hunt is not like warfare
The paradox is that we care
About and for our fellow creatures,
Are one with them in basic features;
We're well aware of this gross irony
For which we make no pat apology.

In killing there's no joy, not a bit;
Without it, no hunt; that's the gist of it.
We claim no territory for all our toil
And without care our spoils will spoil.

Perhaps we might blame Cain and Abel
For our confusing hunter label—
Cain the farmer, perhaps raising wheat,
Abel the rancher, raising sheep—
Farming, though thought more civilized,
Rejected and so roundly criticized—
Spurned for an offering that can be killed
Rather than offering that can be milled.
So that round went the barbarian way
Was it civilized loss? It's hard to say.

It was thought at the time Cain overreacted:
His place as first son was quickly retracted.
It's a terrible thing to "slew" one's brother;
It's a terrible thing to slay any other—
But what is more civilized, to cut a sheep's throat
Or grind grain for bread with mill-wheel and moat?
But Jehovah himself marked Cain from that time
And never forgave him that very first crime.
So humans kill creatures: this meaning was taken

With never a hint that God was mistaken.

So it is then that I presume to take
Some wild creature's life in order to make
A dinner, or find some quaint human use,
Or justify what must appear abuse.
Was it some kind of predetermined fall
(So called) made ready to excuse us all?
Or was it simply nature's mindless way,
Universal force—matter—on display?
No matter. I won't make excuse, blame the past;
Like it or not, this is what I am, and what we are at
last.

Reciprocity

We met recently, I know;
had some small talk—
you had friends in tow—
I'm having trouble with your name,
my fault; I'm to blame as usual,
not being good at short meetings—
but really, casual greetings
of unequals in age and interests—
Can I be frank? I have experience
to thank for my first impression,
which is that I don't match your
self-possession, that indeed
I might be quite boring,
not having acquaintance with
those of your connection—
neither physically interesting,
which is of first importance
(let's admit it) or intellectually
stimulating which is often
second in line—mind you
I don't mind: it's the same with me;
I'm all for reciprocity.

Placing Blame

That "we all make mistakes"
Is a common refrain
For a good many things we do.
For myself, I can always explain;
So I know it refers to you.

Spider

With the sudden light
he took flight across the rug,
small black spider, moving fast—
not fast enough this bug.
Instinctively I stepped on him
and just as quickly wondered why
I didn't just let him by,
this little beast so slight.
He might have done me good,
hunting prey beneath my sight,
if I just understood.
I should have let him go for once,
not smashed him with my ignorance.

Sorting the Past

Except for one, the drawers were full, about—
Everything from greeting cards to old bills
And I resolved to sort them out.

I needed proof of payment for past utilities.
If found I might avoid an arbitrary downgrading
By distant, bureaucratic new authorities.

While I was at it, I thought I'd discard
All that was not current or needed,
A task that shouldn't prove too hard.

Of course, I didn't find support so old.
I found letters, scrapbooks, photographs
Handbooks for articles we'd sold.

I found a departed daughter's manuscripts,
Journals I'd kept, some pieces I'd written,
"Lists to do" before taking trips.

An envelope contains my navy records.
There are fine folders for my college degrees.
There is proof of academic and music awards.

I was careful, methodical, to sort through it.
But so far as throwing these things away—
Someone else will have to do it.

Rocky Road

We live full time in a land of stone,
north and south at either home.
The northern road might well be blocked
at any time by falling rock. Going up or down
our canyon road, we pass boulders large as houses,
stones of red rock posed above us,
set to fall as cliff erodes—in the south
surround our house with stones,
all graded now by size and color (xeriscape
saves water). Hillsides there show dark basalt,
black evidence of ancient flows. Sand fills in
Sonoran spaces. There are mesas in both places,
large flat-topped forms on ancient rimrock;
there is rimrock too in other places.

Both north and south claim the most ancient granite,
earth's basic stone. The south claims it by canyon depth,
far below a normal byway; but actually the oldest
rock is north, can be seen from the highway.
Some residents in both north and south delight
in stone with colors: garnet, agate, amethyst and others.
"Rockhounds" they call themselves when they get together.
They compare and polish and mount what they've found.
In our south such activity employs a whole town.
Both north and south have such steep rocky mountains,
(actually called Rocky Mountains in the northern place),
that those pretending to be wise insist that,

could they iron the landscape, they could double
the states in size. We're at home in our world
of huge broken boulders, and as we've grown older,
feel somewhat cocky—in that, north or south,
our chosen road has not been more rocky.

Fall

I see the signs of fall again;
I breathe the excess oxygen,
Exhaled all summer long I know
By plants in season as they grow.
Therefore I feel especially well
Am glad to fall for autumn's spell,
Find beauty in the colored trees,
A sky so blue it has to please.
Yet I'm pensive beyond reason,
Sad for such a lovely season.
The wind assumes a solemn tone
That makes me feel a bit alone.
I hear the skirr of dry dead leaves.
My fall time thoughts are elegies.

Hanging the Hummingbird

Arrival rite, hanging the hummingbird,
wooden effigy with whirligig wings,
impossibly patterned and much too large
to be anything like the living things.

We've refurnitured the deck:
we're really back now it would seem,
when we find his nail and hang him there
on his usual deck-roof beam.

We have learned by the rattling sound
of his gray metal whirligig wings
the speed of the wind on the deck—
and what too much Wyoming wind brings.

A very rude wind broke his yellow beak once.
We carefully glued him together.
We hung him back in spite of his wound
on a sturdy black fish leader tether.

He's there in all weathers, summertime days,
measuring strong winds and breezes.
We take him down when we head back south:
we're happy to leave when it freezes.

We put him back in his place on the counter,
lock him in with the rest of summer,
our flashy whirligig-winged wind gauge,
our patterned, wooden, yellow-beaked hummer.

Alone at Ten-five

Alone at ten-five, no clouds in view,
I won't need the compass this flight,
Sweetwater River a plain line below me
my green guide to Pinedale always in sight,
Greens on the port wing, easy to see
plains on the starboard, Rattlesnakes too.

Mountains today I've already passed—
Ferris and Shirleys and sheer Seminoes—
were blue left behind me a short time ago.
(Their views from a cockpit not everyone knows.)
I've seen them in summer and covered with snow.
Seen from the highway they don't seem as vast.

Alone at ten thousand five hundred feet
the yoke in my hands in my gentle control,
I float through the air on aluminum wings
see sky and earth too as a beautiful whole,
become unattached from so many things—
without air beneath me could not be complete.

Wind River Mountains are now in sight.
Sweetwater bends away, South Pass shows.
I twist VOR knob to the Pinedale numbers,
could follow a highway, so far as that goes,
or just follow the mountains on the right quarter.
The thing about flying—you must get it right.

Cherokee Seven-one-eight-foxtrot-Lima
on Pinedale approach I announce to the air—
precaution in landing—no tower nearby.
Landings require my utmost care—
most demanding maneuver of those who fly,
no time, no place, for those who daydream.

A "squeak it on" touchdown, I arrive—
earthbound again on a hard straight tarmac—
no turbulence here, no birds eye view,
a quick "turn around"—I can't wait to get back,
open the throttle, tweak the trim too
soon airborne again, alone at Ten-Five.

Desert

Saturday Afternoon

I'm comfortable here now in mid-April, on my Southwest patio
Looking through the golf course greenery, safe from the snow
Content behind the twelfth tee, Superstition Mountains in view
Finch and hummingbird entertainment, temperature eighty-two—
Actually the temp's eighty-three, taking liberties for sake of rhyme
("Poetic license" to me of the most egregious, inexcusable kind)
So said to myself as poet this sunny afternoon, *Lighten up old man;*
You've already outrun some effects of age and the usual life span;
Go ahead, write some doggerel, some meter and other fun stuff;
You've worried old hard truth and mortality quite enough.
So I thought to myself of meter and capitals, stanzas and rhyme
And not hiding them slant, suggested, and internal all of the time;
There's assonance, consonance, onomatopoeia, trochees
Iambics, euphony, metonymy, synecdoche, spondees.
Who knows? Perhaps, if I keep prosody and paradox in focus
I might versify myself, through rhyme and such, to my *magnum*
opus.
I need a jaunty rhythm (not quite regular) that grates on the ear
And regular rhymes too, masculine, not slanted, or cleverly near—
Yet my natural perversity might use something caesura like
Just to confuse the issue, assuming I can find a form I like—
Time to be respectful, traditional like old laureate Bobby Frost
Not time to be Yeatsian, (civilization, gyre and things already lost),
Or perpetually drowning in gloom, like old Anglophile T.S. E.—
Enjoy the mood, climate, and easy living in my new geography.
Besides, you can always remember Homer, Horace, Ovid, and
Sappho
Walt and Emily, A.E. H., E.A. R., even Longfellow and Ed Poe,
Enjoy pious rose moles with Hopkins, or his verses called sprung

101

Ignoring those prize-chasing complainers, pretentious and glum.
(It's obvious now: I'm loafing here, just having fun.)

Too warm for the golfers I guess, none has yet to come through;
I'm alone with the birds, creatures whose every moment is new—
Doves of two kinds, Inca and mourning, two finches together,
House and goldfinch (lesser). Comes with a shout the Gila
woodpecker.
Out on the fairway two black great-tailed grackles compete in
display
For much smaller mates, females quite coy, but now careful to stay.
Say's phoebe shows briefly, overhead today, in fly catcher style;
I expect to see him (or her) again much closer, in a little while.
Finally the resident mocking bird wings in, special among birds—
Flying bird poet, typical among singers who use others' words.

Ah, here come some golfers in carts, a family of four,
Two parents, two very young children too young to yell fore!
I'll sip a little ice tea now, comfortably; it will be hot soon
And try to remember my patio company, this Saturday afternoon.

Verdin

First sensed in moving leafy shadow
Heard then in sharp but modest "chips"
Seen next in tiny, rufous shoulders
Searching bird that rarely sits.
Mesquite and paloverde nester
Bird from spiny deserts formed
Flits next to ocotillo blossoms—
This bird at home among the thorns.

Sonoran Bloom

March is mostly yellows of some kind,
hillsides luminescent, roadsides lined
with sunshine briefly trapped in
springtime striping to Sonoran views
we make special drives for viewing—
the striping mostly bright blooming
yellow brittlebush and desert marigold
along the road; paloverde trees everywhere,
along roads, gilding the hills and washes,
carrying yellow with the rest of March's
blooms all the way to May—like the
myriad sturdy Mexican poppies
growing golden even in the iron ground
near concrete walkways in Arizona towns—
other hues then to find: chupa rosa red,
Penstemen hillsides showing red in kind—
globe mallow, hardy roadside bush
seen early and late, often with apricot hue—
and owls head clover and lupine blue.
(Of hundreds we can name a few.)

Hedgehog cactus cups in crimson cups;
ocotillo flags its flags of nectar tubes
in strange exotic orangey reds—bright
yellow centers, long (stigma?, style?),
complete with hummingbirds and sheen
of mouse-ear leaves of shining green.
Yellow shows on creosote then, modest
beyond most lookers noting, though profuse

(modesty, apparently, of little use except to bees
heard often now in these bushes and in trees).
Sometime in May ironwood trees bloom lilac.
Later still saguaros flower, pallid petals above it all,
white petals, centers yellow, each bloom
a day's worth, or night's worth, needing bats
or bees to bloom so tall above us all.

In time the fruits turn red (we've seen them then)
and have been told some natives come with sotol
poles to harvest its tall fruit, elated still to take
what bees and bats have pollinated.

Ironwood

Unseen until it blooms in May
This hard Sonoran desert tree
So like its name gives sparks they say
Attacked with either ax or saw
Then burns forever after all.
The growing wood combines with sand—
Sand the source of sparks, it seems,
Synergy—wood and arid land
Make a natural calendar
Newly seen copse in lavender.

But more remarkable to me—
Among May's white saguaro blooms
And green-yellow paloverde—
Is the single, lone ironwood,
Lilac beyond all likelihood—
Huge, round, individual form
Dressed in royal lavender
With immunity to harm and
Indifference to you or me
Hardy, timeless, Sonoran tree.

Picketpost

Huge, torn and creased, as solitary as a butte,
The ragged mountain looms before us, near almost—
We've crossed Gonzales Pass in good time on this route;
A sign beside the new paved road reads "Picketpost."

This was Apache land, a stronghold we are told,
The mountain was the lookout point for native scouts.
From there they saw the Bluecoats and could hold
Them off; seeing every movement from this high lookout.

They didn't name it though. The Bluecoats managed that.
They took the mountain for themselves and could see
From their newly conquered mountain plat
Every movement of the now dispossessed Apache.

Not far beyond the famous mountain lookout
The cliff-like side of another mountain shows—
"Apache Leap" its name; and the story is about
Warriors leaping to avoid capture, so that story goes.

Seventy-five warriors leapt with their mounts.
Legend has it that the "Dine'"wept, especially mothers:
(Dine' is their private name by most accounts;
Apache, meaning "enemy," given by others.)

The Dine' tears so shed turned then to stone,
Black, the color of such hopeless grief, bad luck:
A gemstone found no other place but there alone
Today you can buy "Apache Tears" for good luck.

The road then passes through a mining town—
Silver was the first object, then gold and copper;
In other towns along the way activity is down,
But still in view is evidence of stack and hopper.

We wind up then through narrow canyon walls
So close it takes a tunnel to pass one place.
Signs warn us to be careful of rock falls—
And opposite the road one more Apache trace:

The dim outline of an ancient trail, more a path,
Appears to hang against the farside cliff,
Said to be the route for ancient warriors wrath,
It's probable that tale is just a recent myth.

Just outside that upper narrow canyon mouth
Was found to be a world-class copper source:
On our right, a long mountain running south—
Sacred to Apache, mined only with remorse.

The Apache, a proud people, as we know,
Are here still, our destination their new stronghold;
We plan to spend the day at their casino,
Apache place now known to all: **Apache Gold.**

Green Stick

"Green stick" is its name in translation,
Common Sonoran paloverde tree,
Growing wildly in every direction—
Not the shape of the tree you see
In town for shade or decoration.

Their unruly forms defy domestication
Green, irregular branches, thorns—
Yet to desert civilization
Arid adapted native forms
Find a place through customization.

They're shorn of their ancient vegetation,
Branches cut to form a trunk or two
And trimmed to spindly sophistication
Thinned to let some breezes through,
According to the late convention.

These trees are now landscape tradition.
In spring they glow green-gold in bloom.
We see them grow with some elation;
Right now one fronts our home's guest room
And shades its western fenestration.

Estate Sale

Someone has come to this,
a cardboard arrow series on some streets,
"Rosie's appraisal and sales" perhaps,
or some more pretentious business name
with which to greet us bargain hunters and
guide us to the spoils and profit from someone's
earthly toils, nameless, of course, anonymous
except by possessions. Rita's at the desk
collecting ransom from old books, perhaps—
(the best clues to the departed bargains maker)—
or maybe kitchen ware, or couches, dominoes
or brooches.

Tools are popular, cheap, complete with fingerprints
from an unknown user—no extra cost, of course—
paintings second hand through missing eyes are
born about and finally carried out, treasures
at a fraction of the choices that hung them.
And when walls like rooms become empty
among us, we wander there, and wonder now
how accumulated things—possessions
(and sometimes obvious obsessions)—
could leave such a presence, a tangible almost,
in absentia.

Abert's Tohees

Shy at first, furtive in bushes
one masked brown bird shows,
then two, and in quick rushes
mine Niger with firm scratches
ever bolder near our feeder.
Dependable for a week or two, gone,
flown. Where do they go?
I need to know.

Two weeks gone and they're back,
running and scratching
as if they'd never flown. I
should have known. Were
they around when I wasn't watching?
Here's proof nature's perverse:
they've only returned
to ruin my verse.

The Golden Years

Ah yes, the "Golden Years,"
when we identify ourselves
by experience, even wisdom,
rejuvenate old fears, discover
new ones seen in mirrors—
find tastes outdated,
seen, heard, or felt—no longer
related to the latest style;
that is of course, if the ears
still hear, eyes see, mind works,
we find most new things vile.
Body parts get lazy, or ache,
or easily break. We make jokes
or carry sacred books denying
extinction, have sudden insight:
death and sex (and greed)
have been our species creed
all along. We mock the
Ephemeridae in longevity,
identify ourselves by past regrets.
Our distinction is to deny extinction
and find loveliness in decrepitude at last.
We don't die; we pass.

Am I out-of-bounds
my verse inappropriate—
wry not allowed, nor cynical sound?
Should I not note the truth
at the "Golden Years" root?
If you're familiar with geese
you don't have to be told
that the color of gold is the color of poop.

Mourning Dove

I've heard you call from farm to city,
Found your almost-nests of sticks;
In elm and paloverde have seen you paired,
Perched touching on some bough—
In the morning I hear your mourning now.

Game bird too, I've hunted you—
Killed you once—no more.
I'm wiser than I was before,
Know not one of us is here for long,
Through loss and time or time and loss
Have come to understand your song.

Bibs

She appeared one winter season—
Solid bob-tailed cat—
White and black, pretty face,
Large white bib under that;
We called her "Bibs" for the obvious reason.

We don't know why she took us on,
This storm-drain resident at Winterhouse.
Before long she invited herself inside
Not to stay, just to case the house,
And then for a time she'd be gone.

In time she made a home in our grass,
Large decorative mounds in front of our place,
Reserving the drain for danger—
Sometimes local urchins gave chase;
We'd see her duck down drain fast.

We never fed her, knowing we'd leave again.
A neighbor did that; we left water,
Bought a soft bed for the garage
So she could come in from the weather,
The door cracked so she could get in.

She finally sought petting and brushing,
Would even sit in a lap
So long as one wasn't so familiar
As to expect a familiar cat.
Relationships don't tolerate rushing.

Like a puppy she followed us walking
To our mail box down the street.
Sometimes she'd wait at the corner.
She was never under our feet.
She would come when she heard us talking.

She greeted us then every returning
To our seasonal home in the south.
She seemed to know we'd be coming:
Sometimes had a gift in her mouth,
Bird or lizard for the front landing.

Her greeting was stately with great aplomb,
Short tail erect as she strolled along.
We came to expect her purring approach;
Like us, she'd learned to belong.
Then came a fall she failed to come.

Weaver's Needle

A thousand feet of rocky spire,
Tuff eroded over eons
Desert landscape to admire—
Place of gold and murdered peons—

Legend says the spire's shadow
Points out the place the peons died.
And doomed are those that follow;
Still thirty-six, it's said, have tried.

When we view this ancient column
Seen for miles with naked eyes
Our thoughts become quite solemn

That gold is such a deadly prize.

The spire itself is little changed,
Eroding still in desert heat.
We have to feel somewhat estranged
In knowing what its tales repeat.

Tuzigoot

It's a strange feeling, standing there in old stone rooms,
roofs gone, among ghosts gone elsewhere a thousand years,
especially since I don't believe in ghosts—what's there?
Why did they disappear, or are they still here, in pueblos
farther north or on the streets where we might meet, kin
of a kind whose real names no one will ever know.
Why did they go so long ago, yet leave a presence
in the smell of earth and limestone on this modest hill?
Did their marsh dry up, was it some fear I feel still?

I think of them sometimes and wonder about the feeling
I get from hiking up the hill to that ancient dwelling,
knowing of the metate shaped stones and sharp shards
and cotton woven into patterns, feeling attended, maybe,
by a dark-haired child with bright eyes, wise in the ways
of corn and squash and otter. I'll call her *Sinagua-with-water*
since she had a marsh and river. More than once I've stood
where someone stood and looked where someone looked,
mute, in some kind of presence at deserted Tuzigoot.

Natives

Natives claim significance for having been there first,
Insisting all newcomers have always made things worse.
Yet natives walked or paddled through millennia, of course,
Until some haughty mounted strangers brought the horse.
That strangers brought diseases is bound to make us weep.
But strangers also brought the chicken, pig, and sheep.
It's hard to be too certain of the source of all things now:
It's likely that those strangers also brought the cow;
And considering quite seriously the cultures of old time
Newcomers were responsible for a different view of crime.

Many systems of belief have traveled widely too
Predictably conflicting with the native point of view—
The search for plunder rationalized as going on a mission
To enlighten backward natives to another superstition,
Insisting special strange new schemes had conquered evil chance,
And natives could participate if only they'd wear pants.
One doubts the significance of having been there first:
It seems to be a question of what is blest or cursed.
Judging from the records of what's happened in the past
They might have had it better had they only got there last.

Fish Creek Hill

At least fish creek hill is real—
treacherous narrow section
of Arizona's Apache Trail,
up or down nine hundred feet
along a sheer cliff in a mile.

The trail is always "the historic."
Trying to find out why, you feel
its claim to fame is what it might
have been. It might have been
a trade route between Anasazi
and Hohokam. Maybe the Salado
used it (AD 900). Maybe.

What it was, maybe, was
a stagecoach route, except the
only proof of any early use
is in photographs that show
horse drawn wagons hauling
dam supplies (AD 1905).
It's no surprise.

What else is real? Well, when
his namesake dam was done
Teddy himself made the run
and on the way proclaimed,
as was his wont, *the scenery
the most magnificent in the world,*
or something such. (He said the

same thing about the Grand Canyon—
which meant he liked it very much.)

In fact the road, mainly dirt,
became both scenic and historic
because a governor said it was:
tourists liked the view. It wouldn't
hurt to pave it now, let traffic through
without the dust and roadbed bounce
and without the pretence for once.
Perhaps, naming it historic
is ample excuse to pretend
its use means you can't pave it.

I don't know what they'd do
with fish creek hill—ruin the
the thrill, I suppose, for those
not used to running mountain
roads, or the few who don't need
false romance to make the view.
Or is it that unless the road is rough
just being there is not enough?

Great-tailed Grackle

Half tail, il Duce of birds points his long pointed beak to the sky,
transposes a rusty-hinge voice into sweet come-hither bird lyrics,
produces subtle, intricate whistles. He parades his stuff, feathers
glancing purple in the sun, enough color and almost song
to entice the prize, a harem from attentive brownish females
little more than half his size. Once in a while he interrupts
his grackle singing to squat and spread vibrating wings,
arch his inverted-"v"-shaped tail to demonstrate his mounting style.
He does his mating pitch from some high perch or by strutting
on the ground while the brown potential harem follow him around.

Soon enough he's back to his old tricks, villain to the smallbirdhood,
stealing eggs from nests or killing the brood itself, even capturing
and carrying off the tiny adults. Carnivore of opportunity, maestro
of small bird silence, bane to lizards and grasshoppers, and anything
else in an insect brew, this black predator of the yellow eyes can wax
fat on seeds and berries too—if he has to. Outsider, ruffian, hanger-on
to the bird feeder flock, he mocks us with a hunting ground moving
ever farther north, invites us once again to wonder what his kind is
worth.

Time Out

Each day cliché, I'm tired to death—
The only constant change that isn't,
Bored out of mind to my last breath—
I'm done with being pleasant.
The news admits we never learn;
A neighbor's mutts keep yapping:
The reason now I'd have to say
That you won't catch me napping.
I wish the world would go away;
But as we so wisely like to say
Relax, tomorrow's another day.
This too they say: *This too will pass.*
True to my present mood I say
You may kindly kiss my . .
One more cliché that fits my mood
In full, lock, stock, and barrel—
I'm pretty good at being rude
But in no mood for sorrow.
So let it be: *Time Out* for now,
We all get through these times somehow
So check with me tomorrow.

Beyond

Sum

Sum, as in *sum, es, est,*
sumus, estes, sunt,
and is the secret thinking?
Should I defer to Descartes?
Then it would have to be
Je suis in part.
For I have crossed the
streets and come
to *bibliotheque;*
or was it *aedificium?*
Ergo sum.

Epoch

Petrified bones are frequently found.
Ossified forests hold no mysteries for me.
Swamps making coal yet cover much ground.
I'm kin to the bones and the bones' ancestry.

Wholly at one with this bulging time-space,
I'm home in all ages, Stone, Bronze, or Classic.
The ground yet shudders on Earth's granite face.
New bones can be found as huge as Jurassic.

Volcanic eruptions may blank out the sun.
Species in millions, including our own,
Appear and die out to the very last one,
Joining the cycle that turns them to stone.

In me find a full epoch, in you, if you please:
Our dinosaurs sing in the oceans
And sing from the trees.

Ancestors

Rounded stones made of minute fossils
Stromatolites by name
Found at the edge of southern oceans
Hard evidence to explain
From where we came—

Accretions from eons in the past—
Cryanobacteria—
Living cells born of sea and chance
Fulfill life's criteria
Create hysteria—

To imagine all life came from that
Confounds theology—
The universe moves by its own law
Of ontogeny
Without apology.

Order

It might be as leaves violent in the wind,
Seen through a window pane
Or in a soundless motion picture.
Nothing but experience apprehends
A rhythm or a reason as they strain,
Sometimes with the vehemence of rupture.
No sound or sense explains the twisting stems—
Except occasionally the dripping tick of rain
Affirms an insane palpitation within nature.

A Minor Monist

Let us imagine ourselves deaf, dumb, and blind.
Then where is the mind?
Would it remain in the brain
If we couldn't see to project it again?
Would it be real
If we couldn't feel?
Would the darkness be a bore
Without our sensual metaphor?
Must we believe the idea has merit
That flesh is one thing; another is spirit?

Cardigan

Faded a little now
from gray-green to
a little something else
somehow, not too heavy,
not too light (just right),
my favorite extra layer
winter, spring, fall, day
or night—now I am of an age
to match the sagging pockets
with sagging shoulders.
What's the word? Old man
prototype?—archetype?
cardigan type? No, that's not
what I've heard somewhere:
a clue perhaps that I might leave
the word to you; I may come to it later—
I know I have it somewhere—
perhaps in rhyme—paradigm?

Thirteen Lines

Not much given to superstition—
Fridays the thirteenth and concrete cracks
Ladders in the wrong position
Walking in another's tracks—
Have never caused me much concern.
But though my world is strictly rational
There are a couple things I've learned:
One, not to be too deferential,
So lose chances, have ideas spurned.
Disgust is really providential;
An inner anger even worse:
These mean something bad approaches—
Private superstitious curse.

Pets

A delicate subject, pets—
To some human, to some threats—
Pet lovers have a lover's creed:
Pets are furry friends, agreed?
There are pets with feathers too;
Some might learn to speak to you.
And then the finny kind
Comes to mind.

I don't mean to come out rude,
But to be objective fits my mood:
If one finds friendship in a fish
To understand that is my wish.
Companionship from a cat?
Cat people, please give proof of that.
Is it that your cat friend purrs,
Or spends the night out killing birds?

Dog lovers are a special breed
To call dogs family fits their need.
I think that connection fine indeed.
Dogs bark to keep you from harm's way.
They might remember what you say.
They wait for you to come on home,
All for water and a bone.

I have doubts pets feel affection—
Food and safety the connection.
With dogs you help make up a pack.
With cats you give a daytime snack.
With birds you are the source of seed.
Fish get the tidbits that they need.

So pets provide a useful myth;
And I would be most happy if
Our other myths were more like this.

To a Modern Poet

Two kinds of modern poets
the poet said:
prudes and pukes
were all he read or heard.
And I have read your
book tonight;
and though you're very good
with words,
he was right.

And I will bet,
could I hear you read
with typical intonation
something yet
behind the whine
would be topical indignation.

Something Shared

The only thing
that makes a poem true—
when the poem includes me
it must include you.

And what includes you
is as true for the mob,
but in case I prove wrong
I'm keeping my job.

And if you write better
about what is true
what can I say but,
Good for you!

High Ground

The late news lately, heard and seen
As usual short on news and long on mean
Insisted that our mortal foe
When caught be seen a harmless guest
Questioned politely for what he knows
Wined, dined, (and churched) at his request
Converted soon from bad to good—
Then freed with ample means for home:

Not nice to seek strategic secrets
To save ourselves from future harm
Never, ever, employ harsh measures
To discover plots to do us in
Moral high ground our proudest treasure
Moral high ground despite the cost
Ignorance preferred to innocence lost.

Blackberry Storm

The newest thing: cell phone
shown by brother—
can surf the web and
do lots of other things
he said—send text messages,
be read, tell time, find email,
play music, speak, record
notes and archive pictures,
twitter, even make a call—
and that's not all:
This is you, he said.
Unknown to me
he took my picture
with the phone and
showed me me.
(It was not the face
or body in my head.)
Not your best side,
my wife said.
He made no offer
to amend it.
I trust he didn't send it.

InDicktus

Nothing like being profound
Especially enjoying the sound
Of one's own voice and word
As if no one else should be heard
And mounting the charger named truth
(Though already long in the tooth)
Demand unconditional surrender
To reason, no other pretender—
Unconquered I will always remain
No matter who might think me vain
Obnoxious to any right thinking
Demanding my way without blinking
Insisting on my own invictus
By naming my own form *InDicktus*.

A Human Condition

Strange, the feeling sometimes of being finally
inscrutable, harmlessly complete somehow,
happy with smiles for singing birds or special
places, or faces, frowns for minor indignities
like misspoken words, casual with sense of time
as metaphor, or rhyme as reality, wondering
at the quality of one's attention or depth of
emotion, or endeavors worthy of devotion—
would it be too selfish to think oneself unique,
beyond knowing, forever foreign, mind tangled
with feeling, body with motion, abstract with
concrete, certainty with ambivalence—could
another ever know each personal story's
relevance and the mindless stamp of chance?

For instance: morning was boat, afternoon river,
noon mind was widgeons, coots, redheads and
newspaper, talk with Jody at her grill—motel
overbooked with diggers for gold in the near
Rattlesnakes—new owner of ranches, wind power
entrepreneur—sure change in the landscape
of the big lake—part of me now, like the four
buck mule deer browsing trees at Lakehouse,
another morning thing now regular it seems—
and the day young yet—and of the days,
now in their thousands ten, full of T.S's afternoons,
coffee spoons and my true loves and harvest moons,
bornings and dyings, comings and goings—
assimilation assimilating, what of them?

What of them, those tens of thousands of
accumulated days, boytime of horses and hay,
uncles and aunts, sunshine and hail, corn and
cousins, Hardy Boys and Nancy Drew, and
Bible too, father and mother, brother and sister,
violin and piano, baritone and soprano—all
part of you—meaning me, of course—almost all
gone now, along with Santa Clause and Easter
Bunny, especially Easter Bunny, what of them
now? What of the days of youthful frustration,
the mature hours of success and despair got
through somehow—am I egotistical or simply
common at last to know certainly, finally, that
no one can know I was here or there?

And always, always, always the faces, faces
from all those special times and places, like
phantoms in color with smiling and knowing
eyes, moving and speaking—I see them and hear
them at all hours, part memory, part thinking,
images more real than reality, companions
like repeated music heard softly in memory
without ending, remembrances once ours
now mine alone, an infinity of sadness
mine only, only mine for all time, all time—
need I acknowledge or should I insist all this
as metaphor for the human condition, helpless
in feeling, helpless in knowing the coming
dark, too sad , for you, for me, too dark to see?

Poesy

T'was the tuner of cursor o're yonder desktop
Hath holden forever on mind part of me
Wi-Fi hath modem'd my nether floppy
Thither the poesy o' Twenty-first cent'ry

My smartphone doth digital the pixel podcast
Hast broadbanded anew thy slim motherboard
O'r hard drive and cursor, nanometer vast
Thy Linux browser hath transistor hoard

Lo! praise the new graphene Bluetooth and byte
Hold fast to thy Blackberry and tuner
Harken to malware with all of thy might
Yon email might digital sooner

Wher'er thou twitter has analog enou
To disk round silicone (silicon?) aright
And terahertz flash to a drive somehow
Verdictized roundly with thy gigabyte.

Alien

Velvet infinity, soft blackness, glowing cosmic rubble,
stars numberless, I grow dizzy looking up, dizzy riding this
molten iron whirling blue space bubble, dizzy and cold
in the night air wandering swiftly through space and time feeling no
motion wondering at my wondering to find more
me's stranger than one formed of dust and ocean, if hands
like a sea lion's, upright like nothing else, two eyes like
multitudes but no wings to see down with, mulling
what could be more alien in all cosmic space than
Homo sapiens sapiens, species congenitally discontent
its infinity the dream of intraspecies domination, creator
of nation against nation, innerspace blacker than
outerspace, a human race through small time to eternity—
dizzy, wondering why we look there when the alien is here.

99

And here entangled in memory and murderous
belief, flowing lava, libido, and the wine dark sea,
whirling *Ursus major, minor,* and words uncursable,
prophetical *tsunami,* rectal rectitude for masses
rhythmically pounding in new generations, defiant
against tectonic earth and electric skies, simian
prophets, regnant classes, pounding away, penetrating
the impenetrable, defying nova and relativity, exalting
proclivity, *Homo* the wise, pounding, pondering
granite and skies, worshipping bright rocks, station,
hierarchies of gods of hopeless surmise, believing
anything, believing everything, satyrs composing
reality, lighted by belching volcanoes, whipped by
furious radiation, exploding sun, here, *Homo,* the wise.

999

Sapient rarely yet approving the lyre, good company
and home—ancient wisdom by odyssey—dreamer of
dreams in trinity, heir of Silurian slime and celestial
gyre, ambivalent moralizer, beauty, truth and time's
arbiter, innerspace despiser of empty immortality but
Absurd without it, *Homo sapiens* hoping, coping, tearing
love from despair, infinitely curious to see what's there,
discovers reason in rationalization yet acts from emotion
coping, wondering why no why is why, laughing in pathos
crying in bathos, dizzy in surmise looking up looking out,
seeing sky indifferent, velvet dark yet tempting, strange,
inviting—a marvel?—*Homo sapiens* is there, inject in space,
impertinent, bent on saving the human race, demanding
cause and effect, defying the incomprehensible, there—
Homo sapiens sapiens, erect.

Poet

It's up to the world to say you're a poet
our poet said. Despite his wise words
I claim that assessment for myself too.
I don't take credit, mind you.
It's not me, but a muse lives in my head.
I know muses are supposed to be female
But the one that lives in my mind
Allows me to speak male most of the time.
This muse is extremely demanding:
When the words show up in my head
I'm given one chance to get them down
Which means sometimes leaving my bed.
She is tolerant of any perspective though:
Male, female, tone serious, playful, ironic
Verse strict or free, dogmatic, Platonic.
So should you decide you don't like what you see
Consider the muse and don't blame me.
And if you determine that I'm in no way a poet,
I won't be sad, show pique, or surprise:
I'll just pretend I already know it.

Tantalus in Tartarus

I reach to eat or foiled and famished
Stoop to drink and nowhere can I find
The peace of satisfied hunger or excuse
To exercise my natural functions.
If that regal sweetness burst above me
I would waste it in my incapacity,
Nor by giving in and bending low
Can I intercept that water flow on my heart.

Reach or stoop, I can do neither in Tartarus,
But must remain rigid, maintaining my godhood:
A Titan in Tartarus, I no longer know
And am no longer able to care
Whether I feel the pains of hunger
Or the pangs of despair.

Ask What We Are

Ask what we are
that we can bear
such sadness everywhere—
heard in our words
felt in our moods
heard in our music
found in our words
under the music
or seen in quiet faces
under tears' traces—
that we can bear
endless loss, leaving,
endless grieving—
yet laugh—
our laughter
another music
out of the sadness
out of the darkness—
against the darkness—

Ask what we are
that we can be
comfortable lost in space
lost in time
leaving no trace—
imagining beginnings
inventing endings—
creating morality
and immortality—

true believers
to mutual extinction
to laughter's end . . .

Is it that myth
sustains us, promise—
some hopeful lie
to help us die?
Or is myth how
we take command
somehow—
of the interminable
unthinkable?

One Day

The moon rose huge and bright tonight.
Today was warm in bright sunlight.
Dawn came alive in lovely rose.
Magenta mountains graced day's close.

Our mountains showed especially clear,
A welcome sight this time of year:
Recent rains had cleared the air.
It's said tomorrow will be fair.

Rosemary bloom is full of bees.
Our ash is showing new green leaves.
I'm gratified this touches me,
At least for now. Too soon we see
We do not share infinity.

Mythology
(respects to Juvenal)

Is Zeus still on Olympus, Apollo on Delos?
Does Hephaestus limp still; is Hera yet jealous?
Do we walk still on Galilee and debate Karma?
Are our beliefs all in BC, or nearby, pro forma?

Now I recognize belief is not given to fun;
And those ancient favorites have had quite a run,
Employing vast numbers in study and war.
They've been good for business and often much more.

But haven't I seen (on TV) space trips to the moon,
Been tutored on HIV and cures for it soon?
I think I've heard "DNA, E=MC" (squared)
Newton, string theory, and embryos paired.

If we really need myths to keep us alive
For a nuclear age we may want to survive,
Why not make a mythology conform to our time:
The twenty-first century, the century that's mine?

Let's face it, today's vocal prophets and sages
Whose minds haven't yet reached the early Dark Ages
Are hostile to anything of modern invention
That threatens authority of revealed convention.

We live still in a world of mass mutilation
(Especially of females—their gross procreation),
With sanctified brutality, justified in holy text.

Pretended morality creates the slavery of sex.

From Tertullian to Marx and those not worth noting
Perverts, fanatics, bigots, create natural loathing.
But to question their madness is treated as treason—
Nothing so rare to mankind as logic and reason.

Nothing like belief to confuse nature and humanity,
With philosophy and theology to promote the insanity—
Provide tyrants and priests with authority metaphysical.
Of course praying is safer than becoming too quizzical.

I'm sorry—not really, I'm just being polite
Though knowing full well I'm inviting rote spite:
The only response to those mocking pretension,
(Along with some sneering and rude condescension.)

I thought in the beginning I might find some humor
In the popular dogmas that consume like some tumor;
But all I can find is unreasoned gross madness
So I'm left with contemporary secular sadness.

I deliberately meant sarcastic meter and rhyme—
Though obvious, it will be wasted; but I feel quite fine,
As part of my time (though it's far form sublime)—
And I'm fully prepared for the inevitable whine.

Beyond Belief

What's belief but wish?
I don't believe in it myself
in any larger sense—
that is, beyond the colloquial.
It seems to be something
parochial, to be proud of.
Humans claim it with pride,
defiantly, daring challenge,
as if not quite certain;
and some are quick to despise
any who don't agree—
those like me, or try persuasion
or shame or blame, or threat
of death—or defamation.
Then there's faith, seems
interchangeable to me.
I suppose two terms have
some use I can't escape, as in
to believe the depth
of my unbelief
you'd have to have faith.

Fantasy

I'm of the rational kind, I think,
but what I find is that my mind
is more often found in fantasy—
fancy for short—organizing wishes,
correcting mistakes, improving retorts,
inventing reasons, doing what it takes
as a male to resolve the sexual
in something more vivid than anything
textual (madness surely); or all day long
some part of a song plays incessantly,
part of an imagined adventure, or a piece
on the piano I never could master.
The past intrudes too, corrected at last—
in my fancy, of course. (You know,
it could have been worse.)
The future is always propitious,
conforms to my wishes.

Naturally, those who fantasize too much
have been thought to be lazy or crazy,
certified as such, named insane even.
Yet reason suggests that all invention—
not to mention convention—began in
someone's fantasies—in someone history
condemns or admires, just dreaming
his or her desires: someone mathematical
or political, sadistic or artistic, whose
daydreams changed everything.

For most of us, I don't doubt we wear
the most troublesome fantasies out; so
perhaps, one way to explain what seems plain:
fantasies may sometimes be insanities
that help keep us sane.

The Big Questions

What's it all about, this being human?
How big is this universe that we live in?
Is there purpose in our living and dying?
Can we understand; is it worth trying?

Are there deities, gods, one or more?
I have been told there are things to adore.
I have heard all these arguments before.
Pretending interest becomes a bore.

Argument, speculation, come and go—
Each thinker wants to join the show.
I become the intransigent foe:
With an apostate's arrogance say, "I don't know."

That's not entirely true of course—
I know some answers and the source.
I tire of all the lame discourse,
And quit the field with no remorse.

Money

Some think of money all the time
Can remember each dollar spent
Indeed, can remember each cent
I think keeping track is fine
A responsible thing to do
I do that too.

Yet given our country's founding
Puritan, Catholic, Deistic
And other beliefs theistic
All suspicious of money's standing
"Render unto Caesar . . ."—
"Eye of a needle . . ."—

I'm sure you know the quotations—
Greed of the seven sins and such
Suspicion of those who have too much
Piety of poverty notations—
I have noticed on our currency
What seems a curiosity.

(I know this thought unpopular;
I tried it out on some old friends
I didn't try to make amends.)
Am I being too secular
Too particular in this
Finding things amiss—

Am I the only one to find it strange?
Every coin has ample space
For words that seem so out of place?
I know that it's too much to change
And I shouldn't pretend it's funny—
But *In God we Trust* on money?

Who?

Who invented beauty, decided what was pretty;
and left most of us out?
Did whoever it was also decide on ugly
and leave must of us in?
And who invented sin? The gods or men?
Who decided our bodies are ugly,
needing to be hid from view?
Had anyone not taught me
I wouldn't know I was uglier than you.

Who decided sex was dirty, bad, naughty, or fun—
take your pick? Who created smart jokes about genitalia
with earthy names like (right here you can do the rhyme
so I don't unintentionally offend some hick like me,
whose nickname is Dick). And who told us how to do it
and whom to do it with? The gods?—
in infinite number all well hung in the sky or below?
We've been to both places, seriously:
so far, without exception, they've all been no-show.

And who came up with the idea, "gods," countless in
number?—
probably anyone who couldn't answer
or figure it out. Are they all gratuitous fabrication
for some self-serving gratification—a way to make
a superior place in nature for mankind's sake?

Who decided some deserved to rule,
some (most) to submit, especially the "weaker sex"?
Who decided the right to immortality was next
in importance to piety, or that immortality existed at all?
And who decided rectitude could be measured in money?
Seriously considered this all should be hilariously funny—
beauty, ugliness, primogeniture, deities—enough!
All this considered fully, who decides this stuff?

Lapse

I know I came here for something
I thought was in the study.
I'm looking in now thinking
What was it I came in here for?

I came in here for something.
I'm looking in now from the door:
I thought it was in the study.
What was it I came in here for?

It might help if I just look in,
Just stand here and think back.
Between here and where I was
Somehow I just lost track.

I came in here for something—
And I've looked in here before—
I was talking on the kitchen phone—
What was it I came in here for?

Observer

It seems I mostly live outside my skin:
In rare moments only am I found within.
Somehow, from somewhere else I look,
Observe as from a distance one would view
An actor playing someone that he knew.

This may be odd or common; I don't know.
Some think it's what makes a conscience grow.
A mistranslation from an ancient book
Insists a soul is somewhere to be found.
Without doubt other thoughts abound.

My observer is frequently amused,
And knows when I'm insightful or bemused.
He knows that I am frequently mistook;
But never doubts I know what I'm about,
In my skin or when watching from without.

Alma Mater

All Hail! I received your slick alumni
magazine today. I paged through it,
reading here and there. Need I say
it took me back. I thank you for that.
I was reminded through your quotes
from professors' notes of the quaint
language meant to be scholarly:
prolix, turgid, Latinate. You relate,
as usual, your two hundred year status
as a college of the liberal arts, prove
it with articles factual and whimsical
by alumni and faculty. Strange, for
an institution of your age, I find your
"liberal" no longer classical.

I'm left wondering what happened
to the "liberal" of *laissez faire.* I guess
things changed after I was there.
Usual too were alumni notes full
of successes, association meetings,
travels exotic: the general tone I
thought rather careful to be—not
too patriotic. I never belonged to
the alumni association myself—being
liberally educated. I attended as
an independent, left feeling such

associations rather cynical fund-
seeking academe excrescence,
a version of extended adolescence.
I don't really need an *alma mater*.
I think I would prefer an *alma pater*.

All Hail! but no check for you in the mail.

Sonnet in a Minor Key

My endorphins are orphans:
I'm not going to excite them through stress;
I don't like to sweat, and I'm too tired for sex.
Exercise is a repetitive bore; what's more
So are its aficionados. Let me be direct:
I find all those who pretend to like work,
Or athletic things, to be highly suspect—
Those who insist they enjoy getting tired
Improperly wired or, more likely, liars.

We're told to improve ourselves
With exercise and proper diet, propaganda
Without doubt. I refuse to be quiet
About advice so vicious. Diet begins
with delicious. Exercise is eschewed by the wise.

Reality

Just for a change let's be realistic
You, I, and they, are just a statistic
We live on a rock that circles a star
There's nothing out there that cares what we are
The beauty we see in nature out there
Is not beauty at all if we are aware
Those mountains are nothing but crumbling stone
Indifference in granite to all flesh and bone
That wooded hillside of beautiful trees
Is really a forest of overgrown weeds
That ocean of blue with its whitecapped waves
Is nothing more than a lake full of graves
Our history's a record of mayhem and war
And even today we're looking for more
That thing we call love is lust, just face it
So just for a change, why not embrace it
Of course we must censor all rhymes like this
That call into question our invented bliss
Now this is all clear would it be amiss
To ask all you ladies for a long goodbye kiss?

Orbits

We spin in space—
orbit the sun
at a furious pace
while we spin in place.
The moon orbits us
hiding its back;
it changes our moods
by changing its track.

The sun rotates
in the Milky Way
dragging the planets along.
And the Milky Way orbits—
what?—who's to say?

It was not always this way.
But we somehow belong.
Or am I wrong?
Are we alien to force,
get dizzy in orbit?
Are we somehow off course—
out of sync, can't absorb it?

Album

One by one, five seconds long
Our past appears, when we were young—
Strangers in a picture frame,
Another time, through which we came.
I see ourselves in pixel time
In images six pixels fine.
The record there is quite complete:
The faces age as they repeat.
But even as the pictures change
I can't help feeling oddly strange;
I'm numb with thinking I was there,
Seem so detached, so unaware—
Absent, since I don't know when
Were we alive, real, then?

Jessica

Maestro of meds, she sits the chair, as if to play, organ-like,
the area's computer there, extracts an itinerary—then,
blonde hair pulled back on both sides, fastened
by one vertical pin, hair like Hermes the *Hastener's* helmet,
adequate to her bobbing head, makes a quick bee line
to the next bed, no motion lost, no moment lost—
yet makes time to listen, patient among patients,
gentle among sheets she tossed, feeding, pouring, soothing,
lighting a night's too-long hours with a protean energy
mysterious in daylight, weekly sometimes sixty hours.
She is, without question, among the best of her profession,
human defining humanity, caring, caring for, what's more
a stay in the fate of mortality we are fated to rehearse,
caregiver, dynamo in blue uniform, RN, nurse.

Piano Music

I have no words to say
neither plain
nor in clever metaphor
that might explain
the loss I feel—
that world made warm and real
by those in time that was—
is it because . . . ?
I hear them now in music
especially piano
played slow or fast;
the notes themselves
converse and reminisce
in tune with what I miss
and feel at last.
Some speak in treble clef—
in the bass I hear a few
and there are grace notes too.
Altogether in concerto
their music fills my ear
now that I hear.
It seems our ordinary fate
is that we hear
too late.

Anniversary
(occasional)

Wife, whose name translates "a green bough,"
I hope, celebrating our fifty-five years together,
you will not need to do so much bending now.
I may have learned through much trial and error
in all these years to trim the care somehow,
at least enough to bear lightly on age stiffened limbs
we both bear now.

Our world has changed since we first met:
East to West, experiences in life so far apart.
It makes a modern mystery that we are together yet,
going against the grain of modern expectations;
for we have had our share of things one might well forget—
too much compromised mortality in those we shared
a constant threat.

Yet here we are, still going strong,
two pernicious dangers so far defeated still:
I knew that somehow you would make it all along;
and though I have frightened you a time or two
with unexpected lapses too, we yet both belong
to our new way of living, North to South.
For you—this poem.

Snapshot

I paused briefly
To smell the wood chiefly
On a leaf strewn road
In October Maine,
Knowing I would never
Come that way again.

Notice, if you will
The faint smile for you
Before I went over the hill.

Come Dance with Me

Come dance with me, come dance with me
We'll waltz our way to the brightest stars
Make our turnings with the gibbous moon
Dance our way to the planet mars
Learn the new tides of a stellar sea
Come dance with me.

Come dance with me, come dance with me
We'll glide on through the galaxies
Step to the music of the Milky Way
Make our turns through the Pleiades
Through night to light we'll have much to see
Come dance with me.

Come dance with me, come dance with me
We'll whirl to the flashes of supernova
Flounce our way through rude antimatter
Curtsey and bow to time's true Jehovah
Learn what it really means to be
Come dance with me.

A Little Prose

I thought a long time about including a final word, the way I did as an afterword (sic) in my little book *Shortgrass Prairie*. In re-reading that "Afterword" I was pleased to see that I still agreed with myself to the degree that I might as well include it, as I have included many of those first poems, sometimes corrected and "improved" as they now appear. In so doing I run the risk of appearing arrogant or presumptuous, I know, but I'll risk it, being more surprised than anything else at my suddenly making so many new poems (*poet* means *maker*, I understand). But the real reason for putting all these things together is simply that I don't expect to be doing this again; and I have friends enough to appreciate my effort, though they argue against my feeling that this might be the end of it.

Some of these poems are fifty years old. I have made almost all of those after those first published in *Shortgrass Prairie* within the last couple of years, some of them last week, as this is written. I don't expect to make more, but then I didn't expect to make these. (see *Poet*) If there are more they will probably end up in a three-ring binder or as "documents" in a computer.

I consider myself fortunate to have been born in a time and place that related one to a world that barely exists now in our own culture. Many of my early poems recall that world: they reflect, in part, a modest attempt to preserve that time, attitude, language, (as I did in my prose work, *Home*). Nor have I forgotten that time in my later efforts. But one would be mistaken, I think, (modestly, of course) to consider the metaphors or events or persons unsophisticated—being unsophisticated nowadays some kind of shortcoming, though, to me, *sophisticated* seems often a metaphor for pretension, selfishness, and cruelty. At any rate, I think I can say (again modestly, of course) that I have included something for everyone, at the same time immodestly including subjects that the modern sophisticate would find most unpoetic.

As for what a poem is, Robert Frost probably said it as well as anyone in "The Figure a Poem Makes," but he said it so cryptically, it seems to me, that only another poet might "take" his meaning. Therefore I include my own take on the subject, published in my earlier book, as addenda here. In a sense every poem is an experiment: you're stuck with the feeling and form the "inspiration" first takes, and you have to make it come out right, somehow making consistent that feeling and form. Seeing how it all comes out is part of the fun.

RR

Afterword

There seems to be some sort of unwritten tradition that prohibits the creators of poems from saying anything about them—unless invited to a reading or some other literary gathering, a tradition, apparently, based on the assumption that either the reader or the writer is so clever that commentary would be condescending. There have been a few exceptions: at least one member of the school that "got together to shorten each others' poetry" thought it necessary to provide footnotes for his most famous utterance; but even in oral presentations poets often treat their readings as self-explanatory, frequently limiting their comments to expressions of wonderment at their own genius. I am respectful of this tradition only to this degree: I present the reader with an "Afterword" rather than a "Preface." In so doing I stay out of the way, unless asked; but most of the poems presented here have been around a long time, and while I have been gratified by their acceptance, I have been surprised by what is missed, and can see no harm in giving some hints to prove that poets tell quite specifically what they mean, even while the meaning is not instantly apparent, because they give that meaning in metaphor.

First, let me describe what it is I think poems are and what I think they do. Poems are celebrations in the kind of mnemonic music language creates. They preserve a tradition that is both historical and linguistic, at the same time providing immediate experience. They are dramatic performances in which readers or listeners (preferably listeners) participate. They are acts of language. They come in all kinds of forms on all imaginable levels, from verse to doggerel, from the ridiculous to the sublime. As such they have the power to manipulate human emotion from tears and laughter to revolution.

Poets themselves, of course, come in all forms, from the respectable to the reprehensible, from the unlettered to the literary, from the prophet to the propagandist, from the sacred to the profane. There is as much jealousy and snobbery among poets as among artists of any stamp, and while some criticism is informative and helpful, there are whole schools of criticism, many including would-be poets, so full of self-important nonsense and arcane, artsy posturing as to border on the obscene. Robert Frost had his nincompoop (Winters) as the novelist Hemingway had his Eastman. (Perhaps it is better to have a nincompoop than never to be read at all.) Despite the critics, there is no reason one can't enjoy all sorts of poems: sometimes the truly bad is more fun than the good stuff anyway. It is probably healthy to remember that more readers know Edgar Guest than T. S. Eliot. Most poets, even the "important" ones, are remembered by only a handful of poems anyway.

For myself, I have no illusions about creating a "monument more sounding than brass," as did Horace or assuming the role of pious propagandist like a Dante, a couple of references that show how ridiculously self-important poets of all ages can be. I neither want to play as the place burns or stick my head in the oven: my purpose is to celebrate a time and place and language within the realm of my own intellect, tempered forever by that time, place, and language—but not limited to it. I like traditional forms, but have invented my own as well. One who cares about prosody will find sonnets, blank verse, tercets, vers libre, spondees, even a villanelle, one of the oldest forms (which means the title Old Timer may mean more than one thing, you see).* I like to use what many consider newer techniques in traditional forms: slant rhyme is a favorite of mine, as are assonance, consonance, internal rhyme. English meters are really variations of iambic, so far as I am concerned.

Most of all, I assume a reader who will pay enough attention to try a different pace if the first one seems odd and knows when a dictionary might come in handy: it might be absolutely necessary, for example, to know what a scarabaeus is, or to know that "ultima" is always used with another word. The poems may make perfect, and even satisfying sense, without knowing those things; but something will be lost. I was asked once about "granite markers in remembrance" by someone who had driven by "Historical Markers Ahead" signs all her life. One might notice that the bird in Meadowlark sings from a "pulpit," that the windmill is a windmill with attitude, that Coyote has an attitude of his own too, and that Winter Wheat is about something more than winter wheat. The clowns in *Clarification* could (and certainly do) suggest three kinds of folk, you know, depending upon how metaphorically one takes "rodeo." Part of the tradition poems preserve and build on is the literary tradition, naturally, and there are hints of connections from John Milton to J. Frank Dobie—which reminds me: after a reading once, someone mentioned "cowboy poetry." My poems refer to or make metaphors from some of the things cowboy poets use; and if the category fits some of the poems, so be it. Obviously, that category will not fit many of the poems, but I am happy to admit to at least one important similarity: the dramatic voices (persona, if you must) are usually strong, matter-of-fact, and frequently ironic. And so far as cowboy poetry is concerned, not only does much of it measure up on any level, artistic or otherwise, but it is also so popular as to create public celebrations just for the purpose of hearing poets. Wonderful!

At any rate, I would rather my own poems be read with the barbaric yawp of that other poet, who used the word "grass" in his title, than the silly, soulful, singsong of our latest prize-winning laureates, even *Hills and Valleys*, even *Crop Failure*—indeed, though I don't pretend to his art, I would have them all read aloud with the stentorian delivery of that bard who sang of rosy-fingered dawn, heroes, and the wine dark sea.

Shortgrass Prairie 2004
*Also see *I'll See You Still in Every Living Thing.*

Index of titles and first lines